DELICIOUS
DESSERTS

DELICIOUS DESSERTS

Jane Suthering

CONTENTS

ANOTHER BEST-SELLING VOLUME FROM HPBooks®

Publisher: Rick Bailey; Editorial Director: Retha M. Davis
Editor: Jeanette P. Egan; Art Director: Don Burton
Book Assembly: Leslie Sinclair
Book Manufacture: Anthony B. Narducci
Typography: Cindy Coatsworth, Michelle Claridge
Recipe testing by International Cookbook Services: Barbara Bloch,
President; Rita Barrett, Director of Testing

Notice: The information contained in this book is true and complete to the best of our knowledge. All recommendations are made without any guarantees on the part of the author or HPBooks. The author and publisher disclaim all liability in connection with the use of this information.

Published by HPBooks, Inc.
P.O. Box 5367, Tucson, AZ 85703   602/888-2150
ISBN 0-89586-340-5
Library of Congress Catalog Card Number 84-68371
© 1985 HPBooks, Inc.   Printed in the U.S.A.
1st Printing

Originally published as Delicious Desserts
© 1983 Hennerwood Publications Limited

Cover Photo: Nectarine-Meringue Torte, page 50.

Introduction

Desserts are the perfect way to end a meal. Why not invite friends over for a dessert party? You're sure to find a dessert for even the most discriminating palate! In this book, there are five chapters: a *Quick & Easy* section; desserts for *Special Occasions*; *Elegant Desserts* for when you want something unusual; *Baked Desserts* and *Frozen Desserts*. Although there is a theme to each chapter, many basic mixtures, including pastry, meringue and custards, are found in more than one section.

QUICK & EASY

As the name implies, this section includes desserts that can be put together simply and easily. Some are made from fresh whipped cream with added flavorings, such as *Strawberry & Cointreau Cream*, *Scottish Honey Crunch* and *Creamy Toffee Crunch*.

Fresh and canned fruits are easy to prepare and can be served in a variety of ways. For example, canned apricots accompany toasted pound cake for *Apricot Toasts*.

Liqueurs and wine blend successfully with fruits to give delicious results, as in *Banana Flambé* and *Cherries in Red Wine*.

Gelatin-based desserts are always quick and easy to make although it takes time for them to set. Several gelatin desserts are included. Many recipes use ingredients you can keep on hand to make an interesting dessert for unexpected guests.

SPECIAL OCCASIONS

Many recipes in this chapter include the preparation of custards, for which the basic ingredients are eggs and milk or cream. *Crème Brûlée* is a rich spoonable custard with a caramel crust. *Crème Caramel*, a firm custard with a caramel topping, is baked and then unmolded. Stirred custard is the base for *Floating Islands*. A rich egg custard is baked around apples for *French Apple Tart*.

Fresh fruit always makes a good dessert, especially if it is prepared with imagination. *Pineapple & Kirsch Roll*, for example, is spectacular with a fresh pineapple. Fruits can also be made into mousses, fools and whips. Two examples are *Gooseberry Fool* and *Berry Whip*.

Soft cheeses, such as cream cheese, ricotta cheese or cottage cheese, are good for making cheesecakes, but try *Paskha* or *Coeur à la Crème* for unusual variations.

This section also includes a variety of pastries, from shortcrust and frozen puff pastry, to rich sweet pastries and strudel.

Egg white is used in a variety of ways: baked into meringues, poached in milk for *Floating Islands* or simply beaten to add lightness to mousses and fools.

ELEGANT DESSERTS

Some of these desserts require extra time to prepare, assemble and decorate. However, this is time well spent because the results are spectacular. Some are quite inexpensive, using basic ingredients with perhaps a special seasonal fruit. Good examples are *Nectarine-Meringue Torte* and *Kiwifruit Pavlova*, both variations of meringue decorated with whipped cream and exotic fruit. If the fruit suggested in the recipe is not available, experiment with other flavors. Most fresh fruits can be used, or use well-drained canned fruit.

Liqueurs and spirits are used frequently to enhance and complement the flavor of the desserts and to add sparkle.

BAKED DESSERTS

This section includes some traditional favorites, such as *Apple Crisp*, *Peach Cobbler*, *Crepes Suzette* and *Christmas Pudding*. There are also some new ideas for using basic ingredients. *Sweet Noodle Pudding* uses pasta as an alternative to rice in a rich egg custard. *Steamed Chocolate Pudding* with *Chocolate Sauce* will be a success with chocolate lovers. *Lemon Sponge Pudding* separates as it bakes to give a golden sponge top with a tangy lemon sauce beneath.

FROZEN DESSERTS

Frozen desserts are always a bonus when you are faced with unexpected guests or if extra time is needed to prepare a main course. This chapter contains recipes that are served frozen and those that are softened in the refrigerator or at room temperature before serving. All ice creams, ices and sorbets will scoop better if allowed to soften slightly. The exact time will depend on the mixture, but it will probably be from 15 minutes to one hour in the average refrigerator. If the mixture is frozen in a shaped mold, such as *Coffee-Ice-Cream Bombe*, the dessert is unmolded on a serving plate and returned to the freezer to firm up before decorating. *Frozen Zabaglione* and *Chocolate-Rum Cake* can be served straight from the freezer. The ingredients in these recipes keep the mixtures from freezing solid.

INGREDIENTS & TECHNIQUES

Recipes in this book cover a wide range of preparations. The following information will help in producing the best results.

Cream—Half and half will not whip but can be poured over desserts or used as an ingredient to add richness and flavor. Whipping cream has a much greater fat content and therefore can be whipped to soft peaks for spooning over desserts or whipped until stiff enough for piping. Do not overwhip cream, or it will have an unattractive granular consistency. Correctly whipped cream should have a smooth texture. Refrigerate the bowl and whisk or beaters until chilled before whipping cream.

Purees—The quickest and easiest way to puree fruit is to use a blender or food processor fitted with a steel blade.

Press pureed fruit through a sieve to remove seeds and stringy fibers. Or, press the fruit through a sieve with the back of a wooden spoon or pestle. This method is just as effective, only a little more time-consuming, as using a blender or food processor. Cook firm fruits before pureeing. Soft fruits can be pureed without cooking.

Nuts—Remove the tough outer skin of nuts before using them in desserts. Almonds are often sold already blanched, but blanching is easy to do at home. *To blanch almonds,* cover with cold water; bring to a boil. Drain; cover almonds with cold water. Drain again. Remove loose skins by rubbing almonds between your fingers. *For hazelnuts,* place nuts under a preheated broiler about 5 minutes, turning occasionally. Allow to cool slightly. Place nuts in a paper bag or in a dish towel; rub together to remove the papery skin. *To toast nuts,* place under a preheated broiler. Watch carefully, turning frequently. Or, toast in a 375F (190C) oven about 10 minutes or until golden brown, turning frequently.

Pastry—Handle pastry dough as little as possible. Hydrogenated shortening produces a flaky crust and is preferred for most pastry. If desired, substitute butter for part of the shortening to give a rich, buttery flavor. For flaky pastry, cut in shortening with a pastry blender or two knives until the mixture resembles small peas. For a more mealy pastry, cut in shortening until mixture resembles coarse cornmeal. This coats more of the flour with fat. Mealy pastry is excellent for bottom crusts for custard pies or fruits pies because it does not get as soggy as flaky pastry. To bake a pastry shell *blind,* line unbaked pastry with a circle of foil. Fill the foil with pie weights or dried beans. Bake until the pastry has set; remove the weights or beans. Bake a few minutes longer to dry the pastry before adding the filling. Pastry may be partly cooked or fully cooked in this way. If the pastry is to have a cold filling added, simply prick the pastry well with a fork; bake until golden brown without foil or weight.

Steamed Puddings—If you don't own a steamer, use a large saucepan in which the pudding mold can fit comfortably. Allow about 2 inches between the mold and side of the pan. Add enough boiling water to come three-quarters of the way up the mold. Cover and steam the length of time listed in the recipe, adding boiling water to the pan as necessary. A pressure cooker can also be used for steamed puddings. The cooking time will be less. Follow manufacturer's instructions.

Gelatin—In a small saucepan, stir unflavored gelatin into whatever cold liquid the recipe specifies. Let stand 3 minutes. Stir over low heat until gelatin dissolves. Refrigerate gelatin mixture to the consistency of unbeaten egg whites, 20 to 45 minutes in most refrigerators. Then add fruits, vegetables or whipped cream. Gelatin should mound when dropped from a spoon before combining with beaten egg whites or beaten egg whites and whipped cream. This will take 30 to 45 minutes in most refrigerators. If the proper stage of thickening is not reached before adding additional ingredients, the mixture may separate or solids will sink to the bottom. Do not add fresh or frozen pineapple or papaya to gelatin mixtures. They contain enzymes that will dissolve the gelatin. However, cooked or canned pineapple and papaya can be added because cooking destroys the enzymes.

Examples of designs made by piping whipped cream with a star tip.

Unmolding Gelatin Desserts or Ice Creams—There are two basic ways to unmold a gelatin mixture or a molded ice-cream dessert. The first step in both methods is to use the tip of a sharp knife to loosen the gelatin or ice cream around the top of the mold. Then, dip the mold into hot water for one or two seconds. Quickly dry bottom of mold; invert on a serving plate. Or, instead of dipping mold in hot water, invert mold on a serving plate. Rinse a towel in hot water; wring dry. Wrap hot towel around mold. If mold does not loosen, repeat the procedure. It will be easier to center the dessert on the serving plate, if you first moisten the plate with a damp paper towel or pastry brush. If the surface of the dessert has melted slightly during unmolding, return to refrigerator or freezer until firm.

DECORATING IDEAS

The presentation of any dessert is important. There are many different types of decoration to choose from.

Citrus Fruits—*Twists:* Cut a thin slice of lemon, lime or orange; remove any seeds. Make a cut from the center to the outside edge. Twist the two cut edges in opposite directions.

Butterflies: Cut thick slices of fruit in half; cut half-slices almost in half horizontally. Separate the two halves to give a butterfly shape.

Spirals: Using a zester, vegetable peeler or small sharp knife, cut long strips of peel from the fruit; twist strips into spirals.

Julienne strips: Using a vegetable peeler, remove peel from the fruit. Using a sharp knife, cut it into very fine strips. If desired, cover the strips with boiling water; let stand 5 minutes to preserve color and freshness and remove excess bitterness. Drain; place in cold water until needed.

Baskets: Make baskets from whole fruit by cutting the fruit in half, making a straight cut or a zig-zag edge. Scoop out the pulp. Or, make baskets with handles, page 70.

Other decorations—Use small mint sprigs, strawberry leaves, crystallized fruit cut into decorative shapes or coffee-bean candy for decorations. Create a border of piped whipped-cream shells or rosettes, or swirl whipped cream with a fork. Melt chocolate in a bowl over hot water; cool slightly. Drizzle chocolate over a dessert with a spoon or pipe fine lines from a pastry bag with a small hole cut in the end, page 46. Use chocolate curls, page 16; whole, slivered or chopped toasted nuts; caramel chips, page 30; or praline, page 72.

EQUIPMENT

Some recipes in this book call for specialized equipment such as a bombe mold, melon baller or flan pan. The right equipment makes dessert preparation easier. If you plan to make recipes that call for these items regularly, you may want to invest in them. However, there are substitutes. If you do not have an ice-cream scoop or a melon baller, use a spoon. Cake pans with removable bottoms can double as flan pans. Metal or ceramic bowls make excellent substitutes for bombe molds or steamed-pudding molds. Pages 10 and 11 show examples of some equipment used in dessert preparation.

Ingredients used for decorating desserts.

1. Soufflé dish, 2. Springform pan, 3. Metal fluted flan pan,
4. Porcelain flan pan, 5. Ramekins, 6. Bombe mold with lid,
7. Charlotte mold, 8. Cloth pastry bag, 9. Paper pastry bag,
10. Pastry tips, 11. Cherry pitter, 12. Citrus zester, 13. Melon
baller, 14. Small spatula, 15. Coeur à la crème molds and
16. Copper molds

Lemon-Pineapple Mold

1 (20-oz.) can pineapple chunks (juice pack)
2 cups boiling water
1 (6-oz.) pkg. lemon-flavored gelatin
1/2 cup fresh orange juice

1. Lightly oil a decorative 4-cup mold; invert onto paper towels to drain.
2. Drain pineapple chunks, reserving juice.
3. Pour boiling water into a large bowl. Stir in gelatin until dissolved. Stir in reserved pineapple juice and orange juice.
4. Refrigerate until mixture has consistency of unbeaten egg whites.
5. Fold drained pineapple chunks into partially set gelatin mixture. Pour into oiled mold. Refrigerate 6 hours or until firm. To serve, invert onto a serving plate; remove mold. Makes 4 to 6 servings.

Quick Creamy Delight

36 (2-1/2-inch) vanilla cookies
About 1 cup milk
1 (6-oz.) pkg. miniature chocolate pieces
2 tablespoons orange-flavored liqueur
1 (12-oz.) carton frozen whipped topping, thawed

To decorate:
Chocolate curls

The cookies and topping blend together as this dessert stands. This is an easy way to impress guests; they won't believe how simple this is to make.

1. Arrange 1/4 of cookies in bottom of a 1-1/2-quart casserole or serving dish, dipping each cookie in milk before placing in casserole or dish. Sprinkle with 1/4 of chocolate pieces.
2. Stir liqueur into whipped topping until blended. Spread 1/4 of flavored whipped topping over cookies. Repeat layers of dipped cookies, chocolate pieces and whipped topping, ending with whipped topping. There should be 4 layers of each.
3. Refrigerate 8 hours or overnight. Decorate with chocolate curls. Makes 6 to 8 servings.

Variation:
Substitute chocolate-chip cookies or chocolate chocolate-chip cookies for vanilla cookies and chocolate pieces.

Strawberry & Cointreau Cream

8 oz. strawberries, hulled
2 tablespoons sugar
1 to 2 tablespoons Cointreau
1/2 pint whipping cream (1 cup)

1. Slice 4 to 6 strawberries for decoration; set aside. Place remaining strawberries and sugar in a medium bowl; crush with a potato masher.
2. Pour Cointreau and cream into a medium bowl; whip until stiff peaks form. Fold strawberry mixture into whipped-cream mixture.
3. Spoon into individual dessert dishes; top with strawberry slices. Refrigerate until served. Makes 4 servings.

Blackberry Fluff

1 (17-oz.) can blackberries
1-1/2 teaspoons grated orange peel
1 (1/4-oz.) envelope unflavored gelatin (1 tablespoon)
1/2 cup orange juice
2 egg whites
1/4 cup sugar

To decorate:
Whipped cream
Orange-peel strips

1. Drain blackberries, reserving syrup. In a blender or food processor fitted with a steel blade, process blackberries and orange peel until pureed. Press mixture through a sieve to remove seeds; set aside.
2. In a small saucepan, combine gelatin and reserved blackberry syrup. Stir well; let stand 3 minutes. Stir over low heat until gelatin dissolves. Remove from heat; stir in orange juice and sieved blackberries. Refrigerate until mixture mounds when dropped from a spoon.
3. In a medium bowl, beat egg whites until soft peaks form. Gradually beat in sugar; continue beating until stiff and glossy. Fold beaten egg-white mixture into partially set blackberry mixture.
4. Spoon mixture into 4 dessert dishes. Refrigerate 2 to 3 hours or until set.
5. To serve, decorate with whipped cream and orange peel. Makes 4 servings.

Clockwise from top: Lemon-Pineapple Mold, Strawberry & Cointreau Cream, Blackberry Fluff

Scottish Honey Crunch

3 tablespoons regular rolled oats
6 tablespoons honey
Grated peel and juice of 1/2 orange
2 tablespoons whisky
1-1/4 cups whipping cream

To decorate:
Orange slices

1. Spread oats on a baking sheet; toast under a broiler until golden brown. Set aside to cool.
2. Combine honey, orange peel, orange juice, whisky and cream in a medium bowl. Beat with an electric mixer until soft peaks form.
3. Stir in toasted oats; spoon into individual glasses. Decorate with orange slices. Makes 4 to 6 servings.

Pineapple & Kirsch Roll

1 medium pineapple
1 pint whipping cream (2 cups)
1 cup coarsely crushed macaroons
2 tablespoons kirsch

To decorate:
Angelica leaves

1. Remove green top from pineapple, cut top in half lengthwise, reserving half for decoration. Peel pineapple, removing eyes with a knife point. Slice pineapple; cut each slice in half. Blot slices dry with paper towels. Remove core.
2. Whip cream until stiff peaks form; reserve 1/3 of whipped cream. Stir macaroons into remaining whipped cream.
3. Sandwich halved pineapple slices and macaroon cream; place flat-side down on an oval serving plate. Continue to alternate macaroon cream and pineapple until all pineapple and macaroon cream are gone.
4. Stir kirsch into reserved whipped cream; use to frost filled pineapple. With a spatula, swirl cream frosting to resemble pineapple peel; decorate with angelica leaves. Place reserved pineapple top at 1 end as shown. Refrigerate until served. Makes 4 to 6 servings.

Left to right: Pineapple & Kirsch Roll, Rhubarb Mallow, Scandinavian Raspberry Flummery

Rhubarb Mallow

1 (16-oz.) pkg. frozen rhubarb, thawed
1 cup water
1-1/4 cups sugar
1 (1/4-oz.) envelope unflavored gelatin (1 tablespoon)
1/4 cup lemon juice
1/2 cup whipping cream
1/2 cup miniature marshmallows

1. In a medium saucepan, combine rhubarb and 1/2 cup water; bring to a boil. Stir in sugar. Cover; simmer 15 to 20 minutes or until tender. Set aside to cool.
2. In a small saucepan, combine gelatin and remaining water. Stir well; let stand 3 minutes. Stir over low heat until gelatin dissolves. Remove from heat; stir in lemon juice. In a large bowl, stir gelatin mixture into cooled rhubarb mixture. Refrigerate until mixture has consistency of unbeaten egg whites.
3. In a medium bowl, beat cream until soft peaks form. Fold whipped cream into partially set rhubarb mixture. Fold in marshmallows. Spoon into individual dessert dishes. Refrigerate several hours or until set. Makes 4 to 6 servings.

Scandinavian Raspberry Flummery

1 lb. fresh raspberries
About 1 cup water
3/4 cup sugar
1/4 cup semolina

1. Reserve 12 raspberries for decoration. Place remaining raspberries, 1 cup water and 1/2 cup sugar in a medium saucepan. Simmer 5 minutes or until soft. Press mixture through a sieve to remove seeds. Pour into a 2-cup measuring cup; add enough water to make 2 cups.
2. Rinse saucepan to remove any seeds; add raspberry mixture to cleaned saucepan. Bring to a boil; stir in remaining sugar and semolina. Simmer 10 minutes, stirring frequently.
3. Spoon partially set raspberry mixture into a large bowl. With an electric mixer, beat mixture 5 minutes or until light and fluffy. Serve warm in individual dessert dishes. Decorate with reserved raspberries. Makes 4 servings.

Butterscotch Mousse

1/4 cup cornstarch
3/4 cup packed dark-brown sugar
2 cups milk
2 tablespoons butter or margarine
1 teaspoon vanilla extract
2 egg whites

To decorate:
Whipped cream
Chocolate coffee-bean candies

---

1. In a medium saucepan, combine cornstarch and brown sugar. Slowly stir in milk. Cook over low heat until thickened, stirring constantly.
2. Cool slightly; stir in butter or margarine and vanilla.
3. In a medium bowl, beat egg whites until stiff but not dry. Fold beaten egg whites into butterscotch mixture. Pour into a serving dish; refrigerate several hours.
4. To serve, decorate with whipped cream and candy. Makes 8 servings.

Chocolate Curls
The easy way—Use a vegetable peeler; pull peeler across a chocolate block to make curls.
The professional way—Spread melted chocolate on a cool, dry, hard surface. If possible, use a marble slab for this, because it cools chocolate quickly. Smooth chocolate's surface, if necessary; let harden. Holding the long cutting edge of a large sharp knife at a 45-degree angle, push knife away from you, separating chocolate from work surface. The chocolate will roll and form curls as knife edge moves along under it.

Spiced-Apple Swirl

1-1/4 cups whipping cream
16 oz. plain yogurt (2 cups)
Grated peel of 1 lemon
1 cup apple butter

To serve:
Thin crisp cookies

---

1. In a medium bowl, whip cream until soft peaks form. Spoon yogurt into a large bowl, fold in lemon peel and whipped cream. Spoon into 8 individual dishes.
2. Top each dish with 2 tablespoons apple butter. With the tip of a knife, swirl apple butter through mixture.
3. Refrigerate until chilled. Serve with thin crisp cookies. Makes 8 servings.

Left to right: Spiced-Apple Swirl, Chestnut Cream, Creamy Toffee Crunch

Creamy Toffee Crunch

chocolate-covered toffee bars
egg white
/2 pint whipping cream (1 cup)

To decorate:
Orange-peel twists

___

. Place toffee bars in a strong plastic bag. Hold open end of bag securely; coarsely crush toffee bars by pounding with a rolling pin or wooden mallet.
. In a small bowl, beat egg white until stiff but not dry. In a medium bowl, whip cream until stiff peaks form. Fold beaten egg white into whipped cream.
. Stir in crushed toffee bars.
. Spoon mixture into 4 dessert dishes.
. Refrigerate several hours. Decorate with orange-peel twists. Makes 4 servings.

Chestnut Cream

3/4 cup whipping cream
2 tablespoons rum or brandy
1 (8-oz.) can sweetened chestnut puree

To decorate:
Chocolate curls, opposite

___

1. In a medium bowl, whip cream and rum or brandy until stiff peaks form.
2. Gradually fold in chestnut puree. Spoon mixture into a pastry bag fitted with a large star tip.
3. Pipe chestnut mixture into 4 dessert dishes. Refrigerate until served.
4. Decorate each dessert with chocolate curls. Makes 4 servings.

Apricot Toasts

1 pound-cake loaf
1/2 cup apricot jam
2 tablespoons sugar
1/2 teaspoon ground cinnamon
16 canned apricot halves, drained

To decorate:
Whipped cream
1 tablespoon chopped pistachios or toasted almonds

---

1. Preheat broiler. Cut 4 (3/4-inch-thick) cake slices; reserve remaining cake for another use.
2. Spread each cake slice with 2 tablespoons apricot jam. In a small bowl, combine sugar and cinnamon. Sprinkle sugar mixture over jam.
3. Broil cake slices under preheated broiler until sugar melts and is lightly browned. Top each broiled cake slice with 4 apricot halves. Decorate with whipped cream and nuts. Serve immediately. Makes 4 servings.

Clockwise from top: Beignets with Strawberry Sauce, Layered Chocolate Crunch, Apricot Toasts

Crunchy Nut Squares

1 cup all-purpose flour
1/2 cup granulated sugar
1 teaspoon ground cinnamon
1/2 teaspoon baking powder
1/2 cup butter or margarine
1 egg, separated
1/4 cup firmly packed brown sugar
1/2 cup chopped almonds, walnuts, pecans or hazelnuts

---

1. Preheat oven to 350F (175C). Grease a 9-inch-square baking pan.
2. In a medium bowl, combine flour, granulated sugar, cinnamon and baking powder. With a pastry blender or 2 knives, cut in butter or margarine until mixture resembles coarse crumbs. With a fork, stir in egg yolk until dough binds together. Press dough onto bottom of prepared pan.
3. Beat egg white until foamy; brush over top of dough. Combine brown sugar and nuts; sprinkle over dough.
4. Bake 20 to 25 minutes or until firm. Cool in pan on a wire rack 10 minutes. Cut into squares while still warm. Cool completely in pan. Makes 16 squares.

Beignets with Strawberry Sauce

Strawberry Sauce:
1/4 cup granulated sugar
1 cup water
2 teaspoons cornstarch
2 tablespoons brandy
1 tablespoon lemon juice
1-1/2 to 2 cups coarsely chopped strawberries
1/2 cup red currants, if desired

Choux Paste:
1/2 cup water
1/4 cup butter or margarine
2 tablespoons granulated sugar
1/2 cup all-purpose flour
2 eggs
Vegetable oil for deep-frying
Powdered sugar

1. To make Strawberry Sauce, combine sugar and water in a medium saucepan over medium heat. Bring to a boil, stirring until sugar is dissolved. Boil rapidly, without stirring, 3 minutes or until syrupy. Remove from heat. In a small bowl, blend cornstarch, brandy and lemon juice until smooth. Stir into hot syrup; return pan to heat. Cook until mixture comes to a boil, stirring constantly. Stir in strawberries and red currants, if desired. Simmer 5 to 6 minutes. Cool to room temperature.
2. To make choux paste, combine water, butter or margarine and sugar in a medium saucepan over low heat. Bring to a boil; stir until butter or margarine is melted. Add flour all at once, stirring vigorously with a wooden spoon until dough forms a ball and comes away from side of pan. Stir 1 minute or until smooth. Remove from heat. Beat in eggs, 1 at a time, beating well after each addition. Spoon dough into a pastry bag fitted with a large star tip.
3. Heat 1-1/2 to 2 inches oil in a deep-fat fryer to 375F (190C) or until a 1-inch bread cube turns golden brown in 50 seconds. Pipe a 1-1/2-inch-long piece of choux paste into hot oil. Use a wet knife to cut choux paste from pastry tip. Deep-fry 3 or 4 beignets at a time. Deep-fry 1 to 2 minutes on each side or until golden brown. Remove beignets with a slotted spoon; drain on paper towels.
4. Sprinkle warm beignets with powdered sugar. Serve with Strawberry Sauce. Makes 4 to 6 servings.

Layered Chocolate Crunch

2 cups chocolate-cookie crumbs
2 teaspoons instant coffee powder
1-1/2 cups whipping cream

To decorate:
Chocolate lace, page 46

1. Set aside 1 cup cookie crumbs. In a small bowl, combine remaining cookie crumbs and coffee powder.
2. In a medium bowl, whip cream until soft peaks form; reserve 1/2 cup whipped cream for decoration. Fold coffee mixture into remaining whipped cream.
3. Spoon coffee-and-cream mixture into 6 dessert dishes. Sprinkle reserved cookie crumbs evenly over desserts. Top each dessert with a spoonful of reserved whipped cream. Refrigerate several hours.
4. Decorate with chocolate lace immediately before serving. Makes 6 servings.

Variation
Omit coffee powder. Spoon half of crumb-and-cream mixture into serving dishes. Top each with 1 tablespoon strawberry or other jam. Top with remaining crumb-and-cream mixture.

Cherries in Red Wine

1 lb. dark sweet cherries, pitted
1 cup light red wine
1/4 cup sugar
1/2 teaspoon ground cinnamon
2 teaspoons cornstarch
1/4 cup red-currant jelly

1. Combine cherries, wine, sugar and cinnamon in a medium saucepan. Bring to a boil.
2. In a small bowl, combine cornstarch and red-currant jelly. Stir into hot cherry mixture. Simmer 1 minute, stirring constantly. Cover; cool 5 minutes.
3. Serve warm or cold with vanilla ice cream. If a thicker sauce is desired, remove cherries with a slotted spoon; boil liquid until reduced in volume. Makes 4 servings.

Banana Flambé

1/4 cup butter or margarine
6 medium bananas, peeled, cut in half lengthwise
1/3 cup packed light-brown sugar
1/4 cup brandy

To decorate:
Sliced almonds, toasted

1. Melt butter or margarine in a large skillet. Add bananas; sauté until golden and barely tender.
2. Sprinkle with sugar; stir carefully until bananas are coated. Stir in brandy.
3. Bring to a boil. Immediately ignite brandy; shake skillet until flames die. Decorate with toasted sliced almonds. Makes 6 servings.

Variation
Peach Flambé: Substitute 4 to 6 peeled, halved and pitted fresh peaches for bananas.

Brandied Peaches

4 ripe peaches
Lemon juice
2 tablespoons sugar
1/4 cup brandy

1. Dip peaches in boiling water about 20 seconds. Dip immediately in cold water; peel. In a serving bowl, toss peeled peaches in lemon juice.
2. In a small bowl, stir sugar and brandy until sugar dissolves. Prick peaches with a fork or skewer. Pour brandy mixture over peaches.
3. Cover and refrigerate several hours to blend flavors. Makes 4 servings.

Clockwise from top left: Banana Flambé, Brandied Peaches, Cherries in Red Wine, Blackberry & Apple Compote

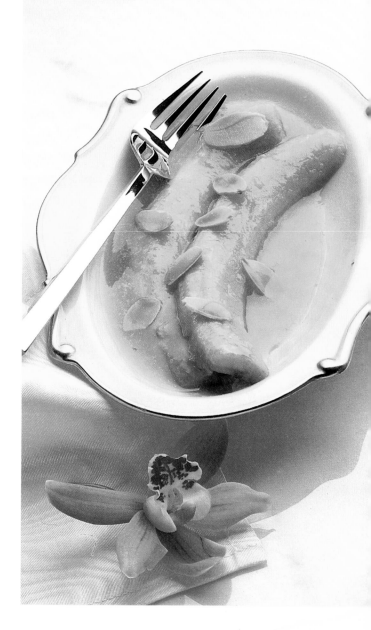

Blackberry & Apple Compote

1-1/2 to 1-3/4 lb. apples, peeled, cored
1 teaspoon lemon juice
6 tablespoons sugar
1 cup water
8 oz. blackberries, thawed, if frozen
2 tablespoons brandy
To serve:
Ice cream or whipping cream, if desired

1. Thickly slice apples. Combine sliced apples, lemon juice, sugar and water in a large saucepan. Simmer 5 to 7 minutes or until tender.
2. Remove cooked apples with a slotted spoon, reserving cooking liquid. Spoon cooked apple and blackberries into a serving dish.
3. Boil cooking liquid until slightly syrupy. Cool slightly; stir in brandy. Pour over fruit; refrigerate until chilled.
4. Serve with ice cream or whipping cream, if desired. Makes 4 to 6 servings.

Variation
Pear & Raspberry Compote: Substitute peeled, cored and sliced pears and raspberries for apples and blackberries. If desired, substitute kirsch for brandy.

Special Occasions

Paskha

1-1/2 lb. cream-style cottage cheese (3 cups)
1/2 cup unsalted butter, room temperature
2 egg yolks
1/2 cup sugar
1/2 teaspoon rose water
2/3 cup dairy sour cream
1/2 cup chopped toasted blanched almonds
1/3 cup raisins
1/3 cup chopped mixed candied fruit
1/3 cup red candied cherries, quartered

To decorate:
Red candied-cherry halves
Angelica
Candied orange wedges, if desired

---

1. Place a sieve over a medium bowl. Add cottage cheese; drain 1 hour. Discard liquid in bowl; press cottage cheese through sieve into bowl. Set aside.
2. Dampen a piece of doubled cheesecloth large enough to line a 5-cup paskha mold or a 6-inch-diameter, 6-inch-deep clean clay flowerpot with a hole in bottom. Line mold or flowerpot with damp cheesecloth.
3. In a large bowl, beat butter, egg yolks and sugar until sugar is dissolved and mixture thickens. Beat in sieved cottage cheese and rose water until smooth. Fold in sour cream, almonds, raisins, candied fruit and quartered candied cherries.
4. Spoon cheese mixture into lined mold; smooth top. Fold ends of cheesecloth over top of mold. Place filled mold on a rack in a shallow pan. Place a small flat plate on top of mold; place a 2-pound weight or a 29 ounce can on plate. Refrigerate 24 hours or longer.
5. Remove weight; uncover top of paskha. Unmold onto a serving plate; carefully remove mold and cheesecloth. Smooth top and side of paskha with a small metal spatula.
6. Decorate with candied-cherry halves, angelica and candied orange wedges, if desired. Refrigerate until served. Makes 8 to 10 servings.

Raisin Cheesecake

2 (8-oz.) pkgs. cream cheese, room temperature
3/4 cup whipping cream
1/3 cup granulated sugar
2 eggs
2 tablespoons grated lemon peel
1 tablespoon lemon juice
1/2 cup raisins
1/4 cup cornstarch
Pastry, page 38, baked in a 9-inch springform pan
Powdered sugar

---

1. Preheat oven to 375F (190C).
2. In a large bowl, beat cream cheese, cream, granulated sugar, eggs, lemon peel and lemon juice until blended and creamy. In a small bowl, toss raisins with cornstarch; fold into cheese mixture.
3. Pour cheese mixture into baked pastry shell; smooth top. Bake in preheated oven 40 minutes. Turn off oven; leave cheesecake in oven, with oven door slightly ajar, until cool. Refrigerate until served.
4. To serve, remove cheesecake from pan; place on a serving plate. Dust top with powdered sugar; score in a lattice pattern with a blunt knife. Makes 8 to 10 servings.

Variation
Peach or Apricot Cheesecake: Substitute 1 (8-ounce) can sliced peaches or apricot halves, drained and chopped, for raisins. Beat in cornstarch with cream cheese.

Top to bottom: Paskha, Raisin Cheesecake

Crème Caramel with Strawberries

Caramel Syrup:
1/2 cup sugar
2 tablespoons water

Custard:
4 eggs
4 egg yolks
1/3 cup sugar
3-1/2 cups milk, scalded
1 tablespoon finely grated orange peel

To serve:
1 pint strawberries, washed

1. Preheat oven to 325F (165C). Grease an 8-inch cake pan or 6-cup ring mold.
2. To make caramel syrup, place sugar and water in a small heavy saucepan over low heat; cook until syrup is golden brown, stirring constantly. Set aside to cool slightly. Pour syrup into bottom of prepared pan or mold, tilting from side to side to coat bottom thoroughly. Set aside.
3. To make custard, in a large bowl, beat eggs, egg yolks and sugar until blended. Gradually beat in milk. Stir in orange peel. Pour mixture into syrup-lined pan.
4. Set cake pan in a shallow baking dish; pour in enough boiling water to come to within 1/2 inch of cake rim.
5. Bake 75 to 85 minutes or until tip of a knife inserted slightly off center comes out clean.
6. Remove custard from water bath; cool to room temperature. Serve at room temperature or refrigerate until served.
7. To serve, run a knife blade around inside edge of pan. Invert custard onto a serving plate, letting syrup run down side of custard. Remove pan. Serve with strawberries. Makes 6 to 8 servings.

Variation

Substitute sections from 3 oranges for strawberries. To section oranges, use a sharp knife to cut peel and bitter white pith from each orange. To free the sections, cut between the flesh and membrane at either side of each section.

> To test a baked custard, such as Crème Caramel, for doneness, insert a knife blade in custard, slightly off center. The knife blade should come out clean. After cooking, always remove the custard from the water bath before cooling. Cool to room temperature or refrigerate before unmolding.

Coeur à la Crème

1/2 pint whipping cream (1 cup)
2 (8-oz.) pkgs. cream cheese, room temperature
1 egg white
2 tablespoons sugar

1. Rinse 6 perforated heart-shaped molds. Dampen enough double cheesecloth to line molds and to fold over top of filling.
2. In a medium bowl, beat cream until thickened. Beat in cream cheese until smooth. In a small bowl, beat egg white until soft peaks form. Gradually beat in sugar; beat until stiff and glossy. Fold beaten egg-white mixture into cheese mixture.
3. Spoon mixture into prepared molds; press down lightly. Fold ends of cheesecloth over filling. Place molds on a rack in a shallow pan. Refrigerator overnight to drain.
4. To serve, uncover top of molds. Invert onto individual serving plates; carefully remove molds and cheesecloth. Makes 6 servings.

Crème Caramel with Strawberries

Crème Brûlée

1 pint whipping cream (2 cups)
1 teaspoon cornstarch
1/4 cup granulated sugar
4 egg yolks, slightly beaten
1 teaspoon vanilla extract
1/2 cup firmly packed dark-brown sugar

Crème Brûlée is a rich smooth custard with a hard caramel glaze.

1. In a medium saucepan, blend 1/2 cup cream and cornstarch until smooth. Stir in remaining 1-1/2 cups cream and granulated sugar. Cook over low heat until tiny bubbles form around edge of pan, stirring constantly. Remove from heat.
2. Slowly stir 1/2 cup hot mixture into beaten egg yolks until blended. Return to saucepan; cook until mixture is thickened and coats back of a spoon, stirring constantly. Do not boil. Cool slightly. Stir in vanilla.
3. Pour custard into 4 (5- or 6-oz.) ramekins; cool to room temperature. When cool, refrigerate 2 to 3 hours or until set.
4. Preheat broiler. Sprinkle 2 tablespoons brown sugar on top of each ramekin, covering custard completely. Place ramekins 2 to 3 inches from preheated broiler 2 to 3 minutes or until sugar is melted. Watch carefully to prevent burning. Refrigerate 1 to 2 hours or until caramel is hard.
5. Immediately before serving, crack caramel by tapping with back of a spoon. Makes 4 servings.

Chocolate-Mint Mousse

5 oz. semisweet chocolate, broken into pieces
4 eggs
1/2 cup sugar
3 tablespoons crème de menthe
3/4 cup whipping cream

1. Melt chocolate in the top of a double boiler over boiling water, stirring until smooth. Set aside to cool.
2. In a medium bowl, combine 1 egg, sugar and crème de menthe. Separate remaining eggs. Add egg yolks to sugar mixture; stir to blend. Set bowl over, but not in, a pan of simmering water. Beat with a whisk 5 minutes or until mixture is foamy. Remove bowl from heat; beat 5 minutes longer or until mixture is thick. Fold in melted chocolate. Set aside to cool.
3. In a small bowl, whip cream until soft peaks form. Fold whipped cream into cooled chocolate mixture.
4. In a medium bowl, beat egg whites until stiff but not dry. Fold beaten egg whites into chocolate mixture.
5. Spoon into individual dessert dishes; refrigerate 3 to 4 hours or until thoroughly chilled. Makes 4 to 6 servings.

Layered Orange Cream

1 (3-1/4-oz.) pkg. vanilla pudding-and-pie-filling mix
2 teaspoons unflavored gelatin powder
3-1/4 cups milk
3 tablespoons orange-flavored liqueur
1/2 pint whipping cream (1 cup)
1 tablespoon powdered sugar
1 (16-oz.) can mandarin oranges, drained

1. In a medium saucepan, combine pudding-and-pie-filling mix and gelatin. Gradually stir in milk; continue stirring until blended. Over low heat, cook until mixture thickens and comes to a boil, stirring constantly.
2. Pour into a large bowl. Place a sheet of waxed paper over surface of pudding to prevent a skin from forming. Cool completely. Stir in liqueur.
3. In a medium bowl, whip cream until soft peaks form. Add powdered sugar; beat until stiff peaks form. Reserve about 2/3 cup whipped cream; refrigerate. Fold remaining whipped cream into pudding. Refrigerate 3 to 4 hours or until thoroughly chilled.
4. To serve, spoon 3 or 4 tablespoons orange cream into 4 dessert dishes. Reserve 4 orange sections for decoration. Spoon remaining orange sections over orange cream. Top with remaining orange cream. Decorate each dessert with a dollop of reserved whipped cream and an orange section.
5. Refrigerate until served. Makes 4 servings.

Lemon-Wine Syllabub

1/2 cup white wine or sherry
1/2 cup sugar
2 teaspoons grated lemon peel
2 tablespoons lemon juice
1-1/4 cups whipping cream

To decorate:
Julienned lemon peel
Lemon-peel twists

Serve this dish as soon as it is chilled; otherwise, it will separate.

1. In a medium glass bowl, combine wine or sherry, sugar, lemon peel and lemon juice. Let stand 1 hour.
2. Add cream to wine mixture; beat until soft peaks form.
3. Spoon beaten cream mixture into wine or sherbet glasses; decorate with julienned lemon peel and lemon-peel twists. Refrigerate 1 hour or until chilled. Makes 4 to 6 servings.

Berry Whip

1 (17-oz.) can blackberries or blueberries
1 (1/4-oz.) envelope unflavored gelatin (1 tablespoon)
3 tablespoons cold water
2 tablespoons fruit-flavored brandy
1/2 pint whipping cream (1 cup)
2 egg whites
1/4 cup sugar

1. Drain berries, reserving syrup. Reserve 12 berries for decoration.
2. In a blender or food processor fitted with a steel blade, process remaining berries until pureed. Press puree through a sieve to remove seeds; set aside.
3. In a small saucepan, combine gelatin and reserved syrup. Stir well; let stand 3 minutes. Stir over low heat until gelatin dissolves. Remove from heat; stir in water, brandy and sieved berries.
4. Pour berry mixture into a medium bowl; refrigerate until mixture mounds when dropped from a spoon, 30 to 45 minutes.
5. In a medium bowl, whip cream until stiff peaks form. Fold whipped cream into partially set berry mixture.
6. In a medium bowl, beat egg whites until soft peaks form. Gradually beat in sugar until stiff and glossy. Fold beaten egg-white mixture into berry mixture.
7. Spoon mixture into 6 wine or sherbet glasses. Refrigerate 1 to 2 hours or until firm. To serve, decorate with reserved berries. Makes 6 servings.

Top to bottom: Lemon-Wine Syllabub, Berry Whip

Gooseberry Fool

2 cups canned, sweetened gooseberries, drained
1/2 cup sugar
3/4 cup whipping cream
1 egg white

1. In a blender or food processor fitted with a steel blade, process gooseberries until pureed. Press puree through a sieve to remove seeds. Stir in 6 tablespoons sugar. Refrigerate until chilled.
2. In a medium bowl, whip cream until stiff peaks form.
3. In a small bowl, beat egg white until soft peaks form. Gradually beat in remaining 2 tablespoons sugar; beat until stiff and glossy. Fold beaten egg-white mixture into whipped cream. Fold gooseberry puree into cream mixture.
4. Spoon into 4 wine or sherbet glasses. Refrigerate until chilled. Makes 4 servings.

Variations
If desired, spoon a few canned gooseberries into glasses before adding the fool.

Mango Fool: Substitute a large peeled mango for gooseberries. Puree mango with 3 tablespoons sugar and 1 teaspoon lime or lemon juice. Continue as for Gooseberry Fool. If desired, spoon some chopped mango into glasses before spooning in fool. Or, place some chopped fruit on top of fool.

Use this recipe as a basic guide for almost any fruit fool. Cook firm fruit before pureeing; puree soft fruit without cooking. Sieve to remove seeds, if necessary. Use about 1/2 cup sweetened puree for 1 egg white and 3/4 cup whipping cream. Sweeten to taste.

Top to bottom: Gooseberry Fool, Mango Fool

Cherry & Cream-Cheese Strudel

2 (8-oz.) pkgs. cream cheese, room temperature
3/4 cup granulated sugar
1/4 teaspoon ground cinnamon
2 egg yolks
1 (17-oz.) can pitted dark sweet cherries, drained
8 oz. filo dough, thawed if frozen
1/2 cup butter or margarine, melted
3/4 cup finely ground almonds
Powdered sugar

1. In a medium bowl, beat cream cheese, granulated sugar, cinnamon and egg yolks until light and fluffy. Fold in cherries; set aside.
2. Preheat oven to 375F (190C). Grease a baking sheet.
3. Unfold filo leaves; place on a slightly damp towel. Cover with another damp towel. Remove 1 leaf; place on a clean dry towel. Brush leaf with butter or margarine; sprinkle with 1 tablespoon almonds. Place second leaf directly over first leaf. Brush with butter; sprinkle with 1 tablespoon almonds. Repeat with remaining leaves.
4. Spread cherry-cheese mixture over leaves in a 2- to 3-inch strip 1-1/2 inches from ends and along 1 long edge.
5. Using towel, roll up strudel, jelly-roll style, patting roll to keep shape. Tuck in ends; brush strudel with butter or margarine. Place seam-side down on greased baking sheet.
6. Bake in preheated oven 30 to 35 minutes or until golden brown. Cool on baking sheet 5 minutes. Sprinkle with powdered sugar.
7. Serve warm or at room temperature. Makes 10 to 12 servings.

> The custard for Floating Islands can also be used as a *Custard Sauce.*

Floating Islands

2 egg whites
2/3 cup sugar
2 cups milk
2 tablespoons sugar
3 eggs
1 tablespoon cornstarch
1/4 teaspoon vanilla extract

To decorate:
1/4 cup whole almonds
3 tablespoons sugar

1. In a medium bowl, beat egg whites until soft peaks form. Gradually beat in 2/3 cup sugar; beat until stiff and glossy.
2. In a large saucepan, combine milk and 2 tablespoons sugar; heat until simmering. Shape beaten egg-white mixture into egg shapes, as shown below. Place 4 egg shapes at a time on hot milk mixture. Simmer 3 minutes. Drain on a clean towel. Repeat with remaining egg-white mixture.
3. In a medium bowl, beat eggs and cornstarch until smooth. Stir in hot milk mixture and vanilla. Strain into a medium saucepan; cook until thick enough to coat back of a spoon, stirring constantly. Cool slightly; pour into a serving dish.
4. To make topping for decoration, butter a baking sheet. In a small saucepan, combine almonds and 3 tablespoons sugar. Cook over low heat until sugar caramelizes. Pour caramel mixture onto buttered baking sheet; cool. When cool and hard, place mixture on a cutting board; coarsely chop with a large heavy knife.
5. Place cooked meringues on cooled custard. Sprinkle with chopped caramel mixture; serve immediately. Makes 4 to 6 servings.

1/To shape meringue islands, use 2 tablespoons as shown.

2/Pass meringue between tablespoons to form a smooth egg shape.

White-Chocolate Mousse

6 oz. white chocolate, broken into pieces
3 tablespoons unsalted butter
3 eggs, separated
3 tablespoons light rum
1/2 pint whipping cream (1 cup)
1/4 cup powdered sugar

To decorate:
Kiwifruit slices

1. Melt chocolate and butter in top of a double boiler over simmering water. Stir until smooth. Pour chocolate mixture into a large bowl; cool slightly. Beat in egg yolks until thoroughly blended. Cool to room temperature. Stir in rum.
2. In a medium bowl, whip cream until soft peaks form. Add powdered sugar; beat until stiff peaks form. Fold into chocolate mixture.
3. In a medium bowl, beat egg whites until stiff but not dry. Fold into chocolate mixture.
4. Spoon into wine or sherbet glasses. Refrigerate several hours or until set. Decorate with kiwifruit slices. Makes 6 to 8 servings.

Variation
Dark-Chocolate Mousse: Substitute semisweet chocolate and dark rum for white chocolate and light rum. Proceed as above. Decorate with orange sections or strawberries.

Floating Islands

Pear & Orange Compote

6 small pears, peeled, cored, quartered
Water
3/4 cup sugar
2 large oranges

1. In a large saucepan, combine pears, 2/3 cup water and 1/3 cup sugar. Simmer 10 minutes or until pears are tender. Drain; reserve syrup.
2. With a vegetable peeler or small knife, cut peel from 1 orange. Cut peel into julienne strips. Place julienned peel in a small saucepan; cover with water. Bring to a boil. Rinse blanched peel in cold water; drain.
3. Cut away bitter white pith from orange. Remove peel and bitter pith from other orange. Slice both oranges. Oil a baking sheet; set aside.
4. To make caramel topping, place remaining sugar in a small saucepan over medium heat. Without stirring, cook until mixture turns light caramel. Pour immediately onto oiled baking sheet. When caramel is set, break into chips.
5. Place sliced oranges and cooked pears in a serving dish. Pour reserved syrup over fruit; refrigerate until chilled.
6. Immediately before serving, sprinkle with blanched orange peel and caramel chips. Makes 4 to 6 servings.

Variation
Tangerine Compote: Prepare caramel chips as above. Remove peel and pith from 12 firm-skinned tangerines. Place 1/3 cup sugar and 2/3 cup water in a small saucepan over low heat; stir until sugar dissolves. Simmer 5 minutes. Cool syrup. Arrange peeled tangerines in a serving dish; add cooled syrup. Sprinkle with 3/4 of the caramel chips; refrigerate 2 to 3 hours. Add remaining caramel chips immediately before serving.

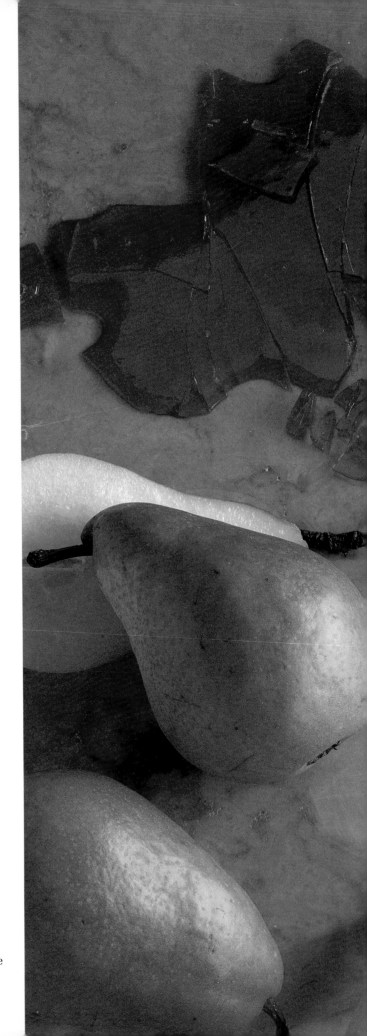

Top to bottom: Pear & Orange Compote, Tangerine Compote

Tangy Lime Mousse

1 (1/4-oz.) envelope unflavored gelatin (1 tablespoon)
1/4 cup cold water
1 cup milk
1/3 cup fresh lime juice
1 tablespoon cornstarch
2 teaspoons grated lime peel
3 eggs, separated
3/4 cup sugar
1 or 2 drops green food coloring, if desired

To decorate:
Lime slices

1. In a medium saucepan, combine gelatin and water. Stir well; let stand 3 minutes. Stir over low heat until gelatin dissolves; set aside to cool.
2. Stir in milk, lime juice, cornstarch and lime peel until blended. Stirring constantly, cook until mixture is thickened and coats back of a spoon. Cool slightly.
3. In a medium bowl, beat egg yolks and sugar until thick and lemon-colored. Beat in warm lime mixture until thoroughly blended. Add 1 or 2 drops food coloring, if desired. Set mixture aside to cool.
4. Beat egg whites until stiff but not dry. Fold beaten egg whites into cooled lime mixture. Cover and refrigerate 2 to 3 hours or until set.
5. To serve, spoon into 4 dessert dishes. Decorate with lime slices. Makes 4 servings.

Ambrosia

2 bananas
2 navel oranges
2 tablespoons superfine sugar
1-1/2 cups shredded coconut

1. Slice bananas into a serving dish. Peel and section oranges.
2. Add orange sections, sugar and coconut to bananas; stir gently. Refrigerate until thoroughly chilled.
3. Makes 4 servings.

Peppermint Pears

2/3 cup sugar
1 cup water
1 tablespoon lemon juice
8 small pears with stems attached
3 tablespoons crème de menthe
Few drops green food coloring

To decorate:
Mint sprigs

1. In a medium saucepan, combine sugar, water and lemon juice. Stir over low heat until sugar dissolves.
2. Peel pears, leaving stems attached. Level base of each pear, if necessary. Using a small pointed knife, carefully scoop out seeds from base so pears remain whole.
3. Add crème de menthe and food coloring to sugar syrup. Bring to a boil. Place pears upright in saucepan. Cover; simmer 20 to 25 minutes or until pears are tender.
4. Place pears in a serving dish. Boil syrup rapidly until thickened. Spoon thickened syrup over pears. Refrigerate several hours, spooning syrup over pears occasionally.
5. Decorate with mint sprigs. Makes 4 servings.

Red-Fruit Salad

2/3 cup sugar
1 cup water
Peel of 1/2 lemon, in 1 or 2 pieces
Juice of 1/2 lemon
2 lb. mixed red fruits, such as red currants, raspberries, strawberries, cherries and plums, ready for eating

1. In a medium saucepan, combine sugar, water and lemon peel. Stir over low heat until sugar dissolves. Boil 10 minutes. Cool; remove lemon peel. Stir in lemon juice.
2. Slice or halve strawberries; slice plums.
3. Place prepared fruit in a serving dish; cover with lemon syrup. Refrigerate until served. Makes 6 to 8 servings.

Variation
Green-Fruit Salad: Substitute green fruit for red ones. Use a combination of melons, grapes, pears, apples, bananas, kiwifruit and green plums.

Clockwise from top right: Peppermint Pears, Tangy Lime Mousse, Green-Fruit Salad

Cranberry-Apple Tart

Filling:
2 cups fresh or frozen cranberries
1 cup sugar
2 tablespoons cornstarch
2-1/2 cups peeled, diced tart apples
1 teaspoon grated lemon peel
1/2 teaspoon ground cinnamon
1/4 teaspoon ground nutmeg

Pastry:
1-1/2 cups all-purpose flour
2 tablespoons sugar
1/2 teaspoon salt
1/2 cup butter or margarine
3 to 4 tablespoons iced water

To serve:
Sweetened whipped cream or ice cream, if desired

1. To make filling, in a large saucepan, combine cranberries, sugar, cornstarch, apples, lemon peel, cinnamon and nutmeg. Stirring occasionally, cook over low heat until cranberries begin to pop and mixture thickens. Cool slightly.
2. Preheat oven to 400F (205C).
3. To make pastry, in a medium bowl, combine flour, sugar and salt. With a pastry blender or 2 knives, cut in butter or margarine until mixture resembles coarse crumbs. Sprinkle with water; toss with a fork until mixture holds together. Gather dough; shape into a ball.
4. On a lightly floured surface, roll out dough to a 12-inch circle. Use to line a 10-inch tart pan with removable bottom. Trim pastry edge even with rim of pan. Spoon cooled cranberry mixture into pastry-lined pan.
5. Bake in preheated oven 25 to 35 minutes or until crust is golden. Cool on a wire rack.
6. Serve warm with sweetened whipped cream or ice cream, if desired. Makes 6 to 8 servings.

Apple-Mincemeat Tart

1-3/4 cups peeled chopped tart apples (2 large apples)
2 tablespoons water
1 (9-oz.) pkg. condensed mincemeat
1 (17-1/2-oz.) pkg. frozen puff pastry, thawed
1 egg yolk beaten with 1 tablespoon milk for glaze
3 or 4 tablespoons honey

To serve:
Vanilla ice cream or sweetened whipped cream

1. In a large saucepan, combine apples and water. Bring to a boil. Cover; simmer 10 to 12 minutes or until apples are tender. Remove from heat; stir in mincemeat. Cool to room temperature.
2. Preheat oven to 425F (220C). Unfold 1 pastry sheet onto a lightly floured surface. Roll out pastry to an 11" x 9" rectangle. Repeat with second pastry sheet.
3. Place 1 pastry sheet on ungreased baking sheet. Spread mincemeat filling over pastry to within 3/4 inch of each edge. Brush pastry edges with water. Fold second pastry sheet in half lengthwise. With a floured sharp knife, cut pastry every 1/2 inch, cutting across pastry through fold to within 3/4 inch of outside edge. Place over mincemeat filling with fold at center; unfold pastry.
4. Press pastry edges together to seal. Using back of a flat-bladed knife, flute pastry edges as shown below. Brush pastry with egg-yolk glaze. Bake 25 to 30 minutes or until pastry is puffed and golden brown.
5. Remove from baking sheet; cool on a wire rack. Brush top of pastry with honey while still warm. Serve warm with vanilla ice cream or sweetened whipped cream. Makes 8 to 10 servings.

Variation
Cranberry-Mincemeat Tart: Substitute 1-1/2 cups fresh or frozen cranberries for apples. In a medium saucepan, combine cranberries, 1/2 cup water, 1/2 cup sugar and 2 teaspoons grated orange peel. Cook 5 to 7 minutes or until skins pop. Add mincemeat to undrained cooked cranberries. Continue as above.

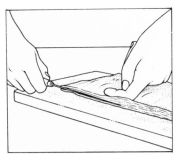

1/Using back of a knife, make several shallow, horizontal cuts in sealed pastry edge.

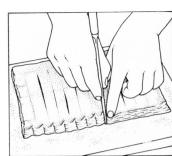

2/Using back of a flat-bladed knife, indent pastry at regular intervals to flute.

Honey Tart

Pastry, page 38

Filling:
1/2 cup honey
1/2 cup light corn syrup
1/2 cup ground almonds
2 eggs
1/2 cup whipping cream
2 cups fresh bread crumbs

1. On a lightly floured surface, roll out pastry to an 11-inch circle. Use to line a 9-inch flan pan with a removable bottom. Prick pastry with a fork; refrigerate until needed. Gather pastry scraps to make a lattice top.
2. Preheat oven to 375F (190C).
3. To make filling, in a medium bowl, combine honey, corn syrup, almonds, eggs, cream and bread crumbs until blended. Pour into pastry-lined pan.
4. On a lightly floured surface, roll out pastry scraps to 1/8 inch thick. Cut 8 (9" x 1/2") strips. Arrange strips in a lattice pattern over filling. Brush ends of pastry strips with water; press firmly to edge of pastry shell to seal.
5. Bake 30 to 35 minutes or until filling is set. Cool completely in pan on a wire rack. Makes 6 to 8 servings.

Left to right: Apple-Mincemeat Tart, Honey Tart

Raspberry Soufflé

2 (10-oz.) pkgs. frozen raspberries, thawed
1/4 cup water
1 (1/4-oz.) envelope unflavored gelatin (1 tablespoon)
1 tablespoon lemon juice
3 eggs, separated
1/2 cup sugar
1/2 pint whipping cream (1 cup)

To decorate:
Sweetened whipped cream

1. Cut a piece of foil large enough to fit around a 1-quart soufflé dish. Fold foil in half lengthwise; grease on 1 side. Wrap around dish, greased-side in, with collar standing 3 inches above rim. Secure collar with straight pins or wooden picks, if necessary.
2. Reserve 4 to 6 raspberries for decoration. In a blender or food processor fitted with a steel blade, process remaining raspberries until pureed. Press puree through a sieve to remove seeds; set puree aside.
3. In a small saucepan, combine water and gelatin. Stir well; let stand 3 minutes. Stir over low heat until gelatin dissolves. Stir in lemon juice; set aside to cool.
4. In a medium bowl, beat egg yolks and sugar until thick and lemon-colored. Stir in raspberry puree and cooled gelatin mixture. Refrigerate 30 minutes or until mixture mounds when dropped from a spoon.
5. In a medium bowl, whip cream until stiff peaks form; fold sweetened whipped cream into partially set raspberry mixture. In a medium bowl, beat egg whites until stiff but not dry; fold beaten egg whites into raspberry mixture. Spoon mixture into prepared soufflé dish. Refrigerate 3 to 4 hours or until set.
6. To serve, carefully remove collar. Decorate soufflé with sweetened whipped cream and reserved raspberries. Makes 6 to 8 servings.

Sweet Shortbread Treats

1 cup all-purpose flour
1/4 cup powdered sugar, sifted
1/4 teaspoon salt
1/2 cup butter or margarine
1/2 teaspoon vanilla extract

To decorate:
1 cup sweetened whipped cream
Raspberries or blackberries

1. Preheat oven to 325F (165C).
2. In a medium bowl, combine flour, powdered sugar and salt. With a pastry blender or 2 knives, cut in butter or margarine until mixture resembles coarse crumbs. Stir in vanilla until blended. Gather dough; shape into a ball.

3. On a lightly floured surface, roll out dough until 1/8 inch thick. Cut out 4 (4-inch) circles. Place circles on an ungreased baking sheet; flute edges.
4. Bake in preheated oven 20 to 25 minutes or until golden brown. Remove from baking sheet; cool on a wire rack.
5. To serve, top each shortbread with whipped cream and berries. Makes 4 servings.

Nut-Topped Cheesecake

Crust:
1 cup graham-cracker crumbs
1/4 cup ground hazelnuts or almonds
3 tablespoons brown sugar
1/4 cup butter or margarine, melted

Filling:
1/4 cup milk
1 (1/4-oz.) envelope unflavored gelatin (1 tablespoon)
2 (8-oz.) pkgs. cream cheese, room temperature
1/2 cup sugar
1 teaspoon vanilla extract or almond extract
8 oz. plain or vanilla-flavored yogurt (1 cup)
1/2 pint whipping cream (1 cup)
1/2 cup toasted chopped almonds or hazelnuts

1. Grease a 9-inch springform pan. To make crust, in a medium bowl, combine cracker crumbs, nuts and brown sugar. Stir in butter or margarine until blended. Press crumb mixture into bottom of prepared pan. Refrigerate 30 minutes.
2. To make filling, in a small saucepan, combine milk and gelatin. Stir well; let stand 3 minutes. Stir over low heat until gelatin dissolves; set aside to cool.
3. In a large bowl, beat cream cheese, sugar and vanilla until light and fluffy. Beat in cooled gelatin mixture until blended. Stir in yogurt. Refrigerate 15 minutes.
4. In a medium bowl, beat cream until stiff peaks form. Fold whipped cream into refrigerated cheese mixture. Pour into crust-lined pan; smooth top. Refrigerate 3 to 4 hours or until set.
5. Before serving, sprinkle chopped nuts over top of cheesecake; press down lightly. Run tip of a knife around edge of pan. Remove side of pan. Place cake on a serving plate. Makes 8 to 10 servings.

Clockwise from top left: Nut-Topped Cheesecake, Raspberry Soufflé, Sweet Shortbread Treat

Glazed-Lemon Tart

Pastry:
1-1/2 cups all-purpose flour
3 tablespoons sugar
1/2 teaspoon salt
1/2 cup butter or margarine
1 egg
2 to 3 tablespoons iced water

Filling:
3 eggs
3/4 cup sugar
1/4 cup butter or margarine, melted
Grated peel and juice of 3 lemons

To decorate:
1/4 cup sugar
1 cup water
1 lemon, thinly sliced

1. To make pastry, in a medium bowl, combine flour, sugar and salt. With a pastry blender or 2 knives, cut in butter or margarine until mixture resembles coarse crumbs. In a small bowl, beat egg with 2 tablespoons water. Sprinkle egg mixture over flour; toss with a fork until pastry holds together. Add remaining water, if necessary. Shape pastry into a ball.
2. On a lightly floured surface, roll out pastry to an 11-inch circle. Line a 9-inch quiche pan or flan pan with a removable bottom. Trim pastry edge even with rim of pan. Refrigerate 30 minutes.
3. Preheat oven to 375F (190C). To make filling, in a medium bowl, combine eggs, sugar, butter or margarine, grated lemon peel and lemon juice until blended. Set aside.
4. Prick chilled pastry with a fork. Line pastry with foil; fill foil with pie weights or dried beans.
5. Bake in preheated oven 10 minutes. Remove foil and pie weights or beans; bake 5 minutes longer. Pour filling into baked pastry. Bake 25 to 30 minutes or until filling is set. Cool on a wire rack.
6. To decorate, place sugar and water in a small heavy saucepan over low heat. Boil 2 minutes. Add lemon slices; boil until syrup is almost gone. Remove lemon slices with a slotted spoon; place on a flat plate. Let stand until cool. Cut cooled lemon slices in half; arrange around inside edge of tart. Makes 6 to 8 servings.

Left to right: Fresh Grape Tart, Glazed-Lemon Tart, French Apple Tart

French Apple Tart

Pastry:
1-1/2 cups all-purpose flour
2 tablespoons sugar
1/2 teaspoon salt
1/2 cup butter or margarine
3 or 4 tablespoons iced water

Filling:
4 tart apples, peeled, cored, halved
2 tablespoons cornstarch
5 tablespoons sugar
1-1/2 cups milk
3 egg yolks, beaten
1 teaspoon vanilla extract
1/4 cup butter

1. To make pastry, in a medium bowl, combine flour, sugar and salt. With a pastry blender or 2 knives, cut in butter or margarine until mixture resembles coarse crumbs. Sprinkle with 3 tablespoons water; toss with a fork until mixture holds together. Add remaining water, if necessary.

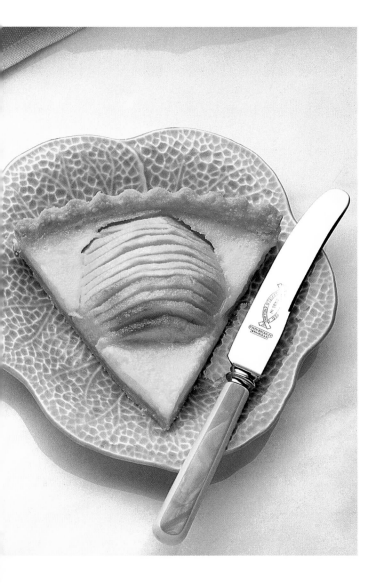

2. On a lightly floured surface, roll out dough to a 12-inch circle. Use to line a 10-inch quiche pan or flan pan with removable bottom. Refrigerate 30 minutes.
3. Place an apple half, cut-side down, on a flat surface; make narrow slashes to create an apple fan, see photo. Repeat with remaining apples. Arrange apples, flat-side down, in bottom of pastry-lined pan.
4. Preheat oven to 375F (190C). In a medium saucepan, blend cornstarch, 1/4 cup sugar and milk until smooth. Cook over low heat until thickened, stirring constantly. Stir 1/4 cup hot custard into egg yolks until blended. Return mixture to saucepan; cook until thickened. Stir in vanilla.
5. Pour custard around apples. Sprinkle remaining 1 tablespoon sugar over apples; dot with butter.
6. Bake in preheated oven 50 to 60 minutes or until custard is set. Cool on a wire rack. Makes 8 servings.

Fresh Grape Tart

Pastry:
1-1/2 cups all-purpose flour
2 tablespoons sugar
1/2 teaspoon salt
1/2 cup butter or margarine
3 or 4 tablespoons iced water

Filling:
3/4 lb. seedless green grapes
1/2 lb. seedless red or black grapes

Glaze:
1/4 cup apricot jam
1 tablespoon sweet sherry

To serve:
Sweetened whipped cream, if desired

1. Preheat oven to 425F (220C). To make pastry, in a medium bowl, combine flour, sugar and salt. With a pastry blender or 2 knives, cut in butter or margarine until mixture resembles coarse crumbs. Sprinkle with 3 tablespoons water; toss with a fork until mixture holds together. Add remaining water, if necessary. Shape pastry into a ball.
2. On a lightly floured surface, roll out dough to a 12-inch circle. Use to line a 10-inch quiche pan or flan pan with removable bottom. Prick pastry with fork; line with foil. Fill foil with pie weights or dried beans. Bake 10 minutes. Remove foil and pie weights or beans; bake 5 minutes longer or until golden brown. Cool completely on a wire rack. Reduce oven temperature to 400F (205C).
3. Arrange grapes in alternating circles in bottom of cooled crust, beginning with green grapes.
4. Bake 12 to 15 minutes. Cool on a wire rack.
5. Press jam through a sieve into a small saucepan. Cook over low heat until jam is melted, stirring constantly. Cool slightly; stir in sherry. Brush glaze over grapes; let stand until set.
6. Serve at room temperature or chilled, with sweetened whipped cream, if desired. Makes 6 to 8 servings.

Elegant Desserts

Strawberry Gâteau

Cake:
4 eggs
1/2 cup sugar
3/4 cup sifted all-purpose flour
3 tablespoons butter or margarine, melted

Strawberry-Cream Filling:
1 pint strawberries, washed, hulled
1/2 pint whipping cream (1 cup)
2 tablespoons powdered sugar
1/4 cup amaretto liqueur

Glaze:
1/3 cup red-currant jelly
1 tablespoon water

---

1. Preheat oven to 375F (190C). Grease a round, deep 8-inch pan. Line bottom of pan with waxed paper. Grease and flour paper and side of pan.
2. To make cake, combine eggs and sugar in a large bowl over a pan of simmering water. Let stand 5 minutes or until eggs are barely warm. Beat 8 minutes or until mixture is thick and lemon-colored. Remove bowl from pan; beat until mixture is cool.
3. Sift flour over egg mixture; fold in flour. Fold in butter or margarine until no streaks remain. Pour into prepared pan; smooth top.
4. Bake in preheated oven 18 to 20 minutes or until center springs back when lightly pressed. Cool in pan on a wire rack 10 minutes. Remove cake from pan; peel off paper. Cool completely on rack. Cut cake into 3 layers.
5. Set aside 12 to 14 strawberries for decoration. To make filling, in a small bowl, mash remaining strawberries; set aside.
6. In a medium bowl, whip cream until soft peaks form. Beat in powdered sugar; beat until stiff peaks form. Spoon about 3/4 cup whipped cream into a pastry bag fitted with an open star tip. Refrigerate filled pastry bag. Fold mashed strawberries into remaining whipped cream.
7. Place 1 cake layer on a serving plate, sprinkle with 2 tablespoons amaretto. Spread with 1/2 of strawberry cream. Repeat with second layer, using remaining strawberry cream. Place third layer on top. Cut reserved strawberries in half; arrange on top of cake, cut-side down.
8. To make glaze, combine jelly and water in a small saucepan over low heat. Stir until jelly melts; cool. Brush cooled glaze over strawberries. Pipe reserved whipped cream around edge of cake. Refrigerate until served. Makes 8 servings.

Variation
Marzipan-Strawberry Gâteau: See photo. Sprinkle a flat surface with powdered sugar. Roll out 7 ounces marzipan on a sugared surface to a strip large enough to cover side of cake. Brush 1 side of marzipan strip with 1/4 cup melted red-currant jelly. Carefully press marzipan, jelly-side in, around side of filled cake.

Strawberry Malakoff

---

1 cup unsalted butter, room temperature
3/4 cup sugar
1 cup ground blanched almonds
1 teaspoon almond extract
1-1/2 cups whipping cream
1-1/2 pints strawberries, washed, hulled, patted dry
2 tablespoons orange-flavored liqueur
2 tablespoons water
7 ladyfingers, split, or other long cookies

---

1. Butter a 2-quart charlotte mold or soufflé dish. Line bottom of mold with waxed paper; butter paper.
2. In a large bowl, beat butter and sugar until light and fluffy. Fold in ground almonds and almond extract. In a medium bowl, whip cream until stiff peaks form. Fold whipped cream into butter mixture.
3. Reserve 8 to 10 strawberries for decoration. Coarsely chop remaining strawberries; fold into butter mixture.
4. In a small bowl, blend liqueur and water. Brush flat side of cookies with liqueur mixture. Line mold with brushed cookies, rounded-side out. Fold any remaining liqueur into butter mixture. Spoon mixture into center of mold; press down lightly. Cover; refrigerate several hours.
5. To serve, let stand at room temperature 5 minutes. Wet a clean towel in hot water; wring dry. Wrap around outside of mold 30 seconds; remove towel. Invert mold onto serving plate; remove mold. Peel off paper. Slice reserved strawberries; arrange around tops of cookies. Makes 10 to 12 servings.

Variation
Fruit and liqueur may be varied according to taste. Substitute fresh raspberries and framboise or blackberries and kirsch for strawberries and orange-flavored liqueur.

Top to bottom: Strawberry Malakoff, Marzipan-Strawberry Gâteau

Cream-Filled Cinnamon Gâteau

Cake:
1-1/2 cups butter or margarine, room temperature
2 cups sugar
2 eggs
2-1/4 cups all-purpose flour, sifted
2 tablespoons ground cinnamon

Cream Filling:
2 pints whipping cream (4 cups)
4 to 6 tablespoons powdered sugar
2 to 3 tablespoons kirsch

To decorate:
Powdered sugar
Cherries

---

1. Cut out 14 (9-inch) parchment-paper circles. Turn 2 (9-inch) round cake pans upside down; grease bottom surface. Place 1 parchment circle on greased surface of each pan. Lightly grease parchment paper. Set aside.
2. Preheat oven to 375F (190C).
3. To make cake, in a large bowl, beat butter or margarine and sugar until light and fluffy. Beat in eggs, 1 at a time, beating well after each addition. Sift flour and cinnamon over butter mixture; fold in. Spread about 1/3 cup batter onto each prepared parchment circle, starting from center and spreading batter toward outside edge. Place pans on a baking sheet.
4. Bake in preheated oven 10 minutes. Cool layers on pans 2 minutes. Invert cake layers onto a wire rack. Carefully peel off paper; cool completely. Repeat with remaining batter to make a total of 14 layers. Layers are very fragile; do not stack.
5. To make filling, in a large bowl, whip cream until soft peaks form. Beat in powdered sugar and kirsch; beat until stiff peaks form. Spoon 2/3 cup whipped-cream mixture into a pastry bag fitted with a rosette tip; refrigerate.
6. Carefully place 1 cake layer on a serving plate; spread with a thin layer of remaining whipped-cream mixture. Repeat with remaining cake layers and whipped-cream mixture. Dust center top of cake with powdered sugar. Pipe reserved whipped-cream mixture in a circle on top of cake; decorate with cherries. Refrigerate until served. Makes 12 to 14 servings.

Brandy Alexander Pie

Sweet Pastry:
1-1/3 cups all-purpose flour
2 tablespoons sugar
1/2 teaspoon salt
1/2 cup butter or margarine
3 or 4 tablespoons iced water

Filling:
1 (1/4-oz.) envelope unflavored gelatin (1 tablespoon)
3/4 cup sugar
1/2 cup water
3 eggs, separated
1/4 teaspoon ground nutmeg
1/4 cup brandy
1/4 cup crème de cacao
1/2 pint whipping cream (1 cup)

To decorate:
Sweetened whipped cream
Chocolate curls, page 16

---

1. Preheat oven to 425F (220C). To make pastry, in a medium bowl, combine flour, sugar and salt. With a pastry blender or 2 knives, cut in butter or margarine until mixture resembles coarse crumbs. Sprinkle with 3 tablespoons water; toss with a fork until mixture holds together. Add remaining water, if necessary. Shape into a ball.
2. On a lightly floured surface, roll out dough to a 12-inch circle. Line a 9-inch pie pan with pastry. Trim pastry edge; flute. Prick pastry with a fork. Line with foil; fill foil with pie weights or dried beans.
3. Bake in preheated oven 10 minutes. Remove foil and pie weights or beans; bake 5 minutes longer or until pastry is golden. Cool completely on a wire rack.
4. To make filling, combine gelatin, 1/2 cup sugar and water in a medium saucepan until blended. Stir over low heat until gelatin and sugar are dissolved. Remove from heat.
5. In a small bowl, beat egg yolks and nutmeg. Stir 1/4 cup gelatin mixture into beaten egg yolks until blended. Return mixture to saucepan; cook over low heat until mixture is thickened, stirring constantly.
6. Pour custard into a large bowl; cool slightly. Stir in brandy and crème de cacao. Place waxed paper over top of custard to prevent film from forming. Refrigerate custard until mixture mounds when dropped from a spoon.
7. In a medium bowl, whip cream until stiff peaks form. Fold whipped cream into thickened custard. In a medium bowl, beat egg whites until soft peaks form. Beat in remaining 1/4 cup sugar until stiff and glossy. Fold beaten egg-white mixture into custard mixture. Pour into cooled crust; smooth top. Refrigerate 3 to 4 hours or until set.
8. To serve, decorate top of pie with sweetened whipped cream and chocolate curls. Makes 6 to 8 servings.

Pecan Pie

Pastry:
1-1/3 cups all-purpose flour
1 tablespoon sugar
1/2 teaspoon salt
1/2 cup butter or margarine
3 or 4 tablespoons iced water

Filling:
1-1/2 cups pecan halves
1 cup dark corn syrup
1/3 cup granulated sugar
1/3 cup firmly packed light-brown sugar
1/4 cup butter or margarine
3 eggs
1 teaspoon vanilla extract

1. Preheat oven to 350F (175C).
2. To make pastry, in a medium bowl, combine flour, sugar and salt. With a pastry blender or 2 knives, cut in butter or margarine until mixture resembles coarse crumbs. Sprinkle with 3 tablespoons water. Toss with a fork until mixture holds together. Shape into a ball.
3. On a lightly floured surface, roll out dough to a 12-inch circle. Line a 9-inch pie pan with pastry. Trim pastry edge; flute.
4. To make filling, arrange pecan halves in bottom of pastry-lined pan. Combine syrup, sugars and butter or margarine in a small saucepan over low heat. Stir until sugar is dissolved and butter or margarine is melted. Remove from heat.
5. In a medium bowl, beat eggs and vanilla until blended. Stir in syrup mixture. Slowly pour mixture over pecans. Bake in preheated oven 50 to 60 minutes or until tip of knife inserted in center comes out clean. Cool on a wire rack. Serve warm. Makes 6 to 8 servings.

Cream-Filled Cinnamon Gâteau

Mocha Pots de Crème

3 oz. semisweet chocolate
1 tablespoon instant coffee powder
1/4 cup sugar
1-1/2 cups whipping cream
4 egg yolks, slightly beaten
1 to 2 tablespoons coffee-flavored liqueur

To decorate:
Sweetened whipped cream
Crystallized violets

1. Combine chocolate, coffee powder, sugar and cream in a heavy saucepan over low heat. Stir until chocolate is melted and coffee is dissolved. Remove from heat.
2. Stir about 6 tablespoons hot chocolate mixture, 1 tablespoon at a time, into egg yolks until blended. Return mixture to saucepan. Stirring constantly, cook until mixture is thickened and coats back of a spoon. Cool slightly; stir in liqueur.
3. Pour mixture into demitasse cups or other small dessert dishes. Refrigerate several hours or until set.
4. To serve, decorate each serving with a rosette of sweetened whipped cream and a crystallized violet. Makes 6 to 8 servings.

Left to right: Cream-Filled Nut Roll, Mocha Pots de Crème

Cream-Filled Nut Roll

Cake:
1/2 cup sugar
3 eggs
2/3 cup ground toasted hazelnuts or almonds
2 tablespoons whole-wheat flour
Superfine sugar

Filling:
1/2 pint whipping cream (1 cup)
2 tablespoons powdered sugar
1 teaspoon vanilla extract
1/2 pint fresh raspberries or blackberries

1. Preheat oven to 400F (205C). Grease a 13" x 9" baking pan. Line pan with waxed paper; grease paper.
2. To make cake, combine 1/2 cup sugar and eggs in a medium bowl; set bowl over a pan of simmering water. Let stand 5 minutes or until eggs are barely warm. Beat 8 minutes or until mixture is thick and lemon-colored. Remove bowl from heat; beat until mixture is cool. Fold in ground nuts and flour. Spread mixture in prepared pan.
3. Bake in preheated oven 10 to 12 minutes or until cake springs back when touched. Sprinkle a thin towel with 2 tablespoons superfine sugar. Invert cake onto sugared towel. Remove pan; peel off paper. Roll up cake in sugared towel, jelly-roll style. Cool rolled cake, seam-side down, on a wire rack.
4. To make filling, in a medium bowl, whip cream until soft peaks form. Beat in sugar and vanilla until stiff peaks form. Spoon 3/4 cup whipped-cream mixture into a pastry bag fitted with an open star tip; refrigerate.
5. Unroll cake; spread remaining whipped-cream mixture over cake to within 1/2 inch of outside edges. Set aside 6 berries for decoration. Scatter remaining berries over cream filling. Carefully roll cake to enclose filling.
6. Place filled cake, seam-side down, on a flat serving plate. Sprinkle lightly with superfine sugar. Decorate with reserved whipped cream and reserved berries. Refrigerate until served. Makes 6 servings.

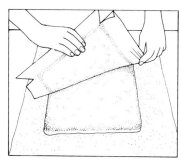

1/Invert cake onto sugared towel. Remove pan; peel off paper.

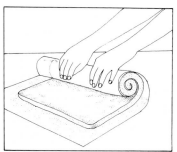

2/Roll up cake in sugared towel, jelly-roll style.

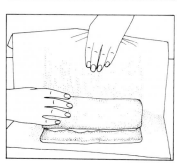

3/Carefully roll cake to enclose filling.

Ginger & Cream Bavarian

1/2 cup sugar
1 (1/4-oz.) envelope unflavored gelatin (1 tablespoon)
3 eggs, separated
1-1/2 cups milk
2 tablespoons orange juice
1/2 pint whipping cream (1 cup)
1/4 cup orange-flavored liqueur
1/3 cup coarsely chopped stem ginger
    preserved in syrup

To decorate:
Sweetened whipped cream
Orange-peel strips

1. Stir sugar and gelatin together in a medium saucepan. In a medium bowl, beat egg yolks, milk and orange juice until blended. Slowly stir into gelatin mixture. Over low heat, stir until mixture thickens and coats back of a spoon. Pour into a large bowl; cool to room temperature. Refrigerate until mixture mounds when dropped from a spoon.
2. In a medium bowl, whip cream until soft peaks form. Add liqueur; beat until stiff peaks form. Fold whipped-cream mixture into partially set gelatin mixture.
3. In a medium bowl, beat egg whites until stiff but not dry. Fold beaten egg whites into gelatin mixture. Fold in preserved ginger.
4. Rinse a 1-1/2-quart charlotte or decorative mold with water. Spoon bavarian mixture into rinsed mold; smooth top. Refrigerate 3 to 4 hours or until set.
5. To serve, invert on a serving plate; remove mold. Pipe whipped cream around bottom and top of bavarian; decorate with orange-peel strips. Makes 6 servings.

Cream-Filled Chocolate Roll

Cake:
6 oz. semisweet chocolate
3 tablespoons water
5 eggs, separated
1/2 cup granulated sugar
1/4 cup sifted all-purpose flour
Powdered sugar

Filling:
1-1/2 cups whipping cream
2 tablespoons powdered sugar
1 teaspoon vanilla extract

To decorate:
Chocolate lace, see illustration opposite

The texture of this cake is similar to a mousse; therefore, it will crack when rolled.

1. Preheat oven to 350F (175C). Grease a 15" x 10" jelly-roll pan. Line greased pan with waxed paper; grease paper.
2. In a small saucepan, stir chocolate and water over low heat until chocolate is melted and mixture is smooth. Set aside to cool.

3. In a large bowl, beat egg yolks and granulated sugar 10 minutes or until thick and lemon-colored. Stir in cooled chocolate mixture until blended. Fold in flour.
4. In a medium bowl, beat egg whites until stiff but not dry; fold into chocolate mixture. Pour into prepared pan; spread evenly.
5. Bake in preheated oven 18 to 20 minutes or until firm. Cover baked cake with a damp towel. Cool on a wire rack until completely cool.
6. Lightly sprinkle a dry towel with powdered sugar. Invert cooled cake onto sugared towel; peel off paper.
7. To make filling, in a medium bowl, whip cream until soft peaks form. Beat in powdered sugar and vanilla; beat until stiff peaks form. Spoon 1-1/2 cups whipped cream into a pastry bag fitted with an open star tip; refrigerate.
8. Spread remaining whipped cream over cake to within 1/2 inch of edges. Using towel, roll up cake, jelly-roll style. Place filled cake on a serving plate, seam-side down. Cake will crack when rolled. Pipe reserved whipped cream over cake. Decorate with chocolate lace. Refrigerate until served. Makes 6 to 8 servings.

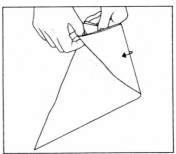

1/Fold a 10-inch square of parchment paper in half diagonally. Holding long side of triangle away from you, bring left corner to middle corner.

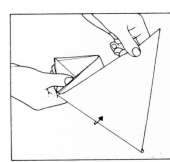

2/Bring other corner around cone, pulling it tight to form a sharp tip.

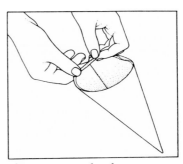

3/Fasten pastry bag by tucking corners inside; make a double fold.

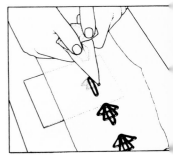

4/Fill pastry bag with melted chocolate. Cut off tip of bag. Place design under a sheet of waxed paper. Trace design to form chocolate lace. When chocolate is firm, remove from paper.

Top to bottom: Ginger & Cream Bavarian, Cream-Filled Chocolate Roll

Gâteau Pithiviers

1/2 cup granulated sugar
1 cup ground almonds
1/4 cup butter, room temperature
2 egg yolks
2 tablespoons dark rum
1 (17-1/2-oz.) pkg. frozen puff pastry, thawed
Powdered sugar

1. Preheat oven to 400F (205C). In a medium bowl, beat granulated sugar, almonds, butter, egg yolks and rum until blended; set aside.
2. On a lightly floured surface, flatten each pastry sheet. Cut out 1 (9-1/2-inch) circle from each pastry sheet.
3. Place 1 pastry circle on an ungreased baking sheet. Spread filling over pastry to within 3/4 inch of edge. Brush pastry edge with water.
4. Make 8 crescent-shaped cuts in top of remaining pastry sheet. Start at center and cut to within 1 inch of pastry edge, as shown. Place pastry over filling; lightly press edges together to seal. Crimp and flute pastry edge, page 34.

5. Bake in preheated oven 20 minutes. Remove from oven; dust top with powdered sugar. Bake 5 to 10 minutes longer or until sugar is melted. Cool on baking sheet 5 minutes. Remove from baking sheet; cool completely on a wire rack. Makes 6 to 8 servings.

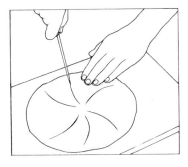

1/Make 8 crescent-shaped cuts in top pastry sheet.

Left to right: Gâteau Saint Honoré, Gâteau Pithiviers

Gâteau Saint Honoré

Pastry Base:
2/3 cup all-purpose flour, sifted
2 tablespoons sugar
1/4 cup butter

Pastry Cream:
2 tablespoons all-purpose flour
2 tablespoons cornstarch
1/4 cup sugar
1-1/4 cups milk
2 egg yolks, slightly beaten
1/2 teaspoon vanilla extract

Choux Paste:
1/2 cup water
2 teaspoons sugar
Pinch salt
1/4 cup butter
1/2 cup all-purpose flour, sifted
2 eggs

Caramel:
1 cup sugar
1/2 cup water

Whipped-Cream Filling:
1 cup whipping cream
1 tablespoon powdered sugar
1 to 2 tablespoons sweet sherry

To decorate:
Chopped pistachios

1. Preheat oven to 350F (175C). Grease a baking sheet. To make pastry base, in a medium bowl, combine flour and sugar. With a pastry blender or 2 knives, cut in butter until mixture resembles coarse crumbs. Shape into a ball. On a lightly floured surface, roll out dough to a 9-inch circle. Prick well with a fork. Place on greased baking sheet. Bake in preheated oven 20 minutes or until golden. Remove from baking sheet; cool on a wire rack.

2. To make pastry cream, in a medium saucepan, blend flour, cornstarch and sugar. Stir in milk until blended. Stir over low heat until thickened and smooth. Stir about 3 tablespoons hot milk mixture into egg yolks until blended. Pour back into saucepan; cook until thickened, stirring constantly. Do not boil. Remove from heat; stir in vanilla. Place a sheet of waxed paper over pastry cream to prevent film from forming. Cool to room temperature. Refrigerate until needed.

3. Preheat oven to 400F (205C). Grease a baking sheet. To make choux paste, combine water, sugar, salt and butter in a medium saucepan. Bring to a boil. Add flour all at once; stir with a wooden spoon until dough forms a ball and comes away from side of pan. Remove from heat. Beat in eggs, 1 at a time, beating well after each addition. Beat until smooth. Spoon dough into a pastry bag fitted with a plain tip. Pipe out 12 to 14 small balls onto greased baking sheet. With remaining choux paste, pipe out an 8-inch ring. Bake in preheated oven 20 to 25 minutes or until golden. Remove from baking sheet; cool on a wire rack.

4. To complete gâteau, place pastry base on a serving plate. Cut cooled ring in half crosswise; place bottom of ring on top of baked pastry base. Spoon chilled pastry cream into ring bottom; cover with ring top.

5. To prepare caramel, place sugar and water in a small saucepan over low heat. Stir until syrup caramelizes. Remove from heat.

6. Dip each choux ball into caramel; place on outside edge of choux ring. Spoon any remaining caramel over balls.

7. To make whipped-cream filling, in a medium bowl, whip cream until soft peaks form. Beat in powdered sugar and sherry to taste; beat until stiff peaks form. Fill center of ring with filling. Sprinkle with pistachios; refrigerate until served. Makes 6 to 8 servings.

Nectarine-Meringue Torte

6 egg whites
1/4 teaspoon cream of tartar
1-1/2 cups superfine sugar
1/3 cup ground toasted almonds or hazelnuts
1 pint whipping cream (2 cups)
3 to 4 tablespoons powdered sugar
5 or 6 nectarines, sliced

1. Preheat oven to 200F (95C). Line a large baking sheet with parchment paper. Draw 3 (9-inch) circles on paper-lined baking sheet. Use 2 baking sheets, if necessary.
2. In a mixer bowl, beat egg whites and cream of tartar with an electric mixer at high speed until soft peaks form. Gradually beat in superfine sugar; beat until stiff and glossy. Fold in nuts.
3. Spoon meringue into a pastry bag fitted with a large plain tip. Pipe out meringue into 3 spirals. Start at center of each circle drawn on parchment paper; continue piping until each circle is complete.
4. Bake in preheated oven 2 hours or until meringues are crisp and dry. Cool completely on baking sheet on a wire rack. Carefully peel off paper.
5. In a medium bowl, whip cream until soft peaks form. Beat in powdered sugar; beat until stiff peaks form. Place 1 meringue layer on a flat serving plate; spread with 1/3 of whipped cream. Arrange 1/3 of nectarine slices on cream.
6. Place second meringue layer on a flat surface; spread with second 1/3 of whipped cream; top with second 1/3 of nectarine slices. Carefully place second covered meringue layer on top of first layer. Top with remaining layer; arrange remaining nectarine slices in center of top layer.
7. Spoon dollops of remaining whipped cream around nectarine slices. Serve immediately. Makes 10 to 12 servings.

Variation
Substitute another fruit for nectarines. Raspberries are excellent served this way.

Meringues are simple to make if a few basic rules are followed.

Bowls and whisks or beaters must be clean and free from grease. Grease prevents egg whites from beating to their full volume. Since egg yolks contain fat, be sure that egg whites do not contain any yolk.

A pinch of salt or a squeeze of lemon juice or cream of tartar will help stabilize beaten egg whites.

Beat egg whites until stiff but not dry. Overbeaten egg whites lose volume and deflate when folded into other ingredients. Beat in about 1 tablespoon sugar at a time, beating well between each addition. Beat until the meringue is thick, white and glossy. After egg whites are beaten, fold in any extra ingredients, such as ground nuts.

Meringues are usually baked in a slow oven one to three hours.

Store hard meringues in a cool dry place. Wrapped in foil or stored in a rigid plastic container, hard meringues will keep at least a week.

Nectarine-Meringue Torte

Coffee-Cream & Meringue Sandwiches

4 egg whites
1-1/4 cups sugar
1/2 cup hazelnuts or almonds, finely ground
1-1/4 cups whipping cream
2 teaspoons instant coffee powder,
    dissolved in 1 teaspoon boiling water

To decorate:
Chocolate curls, page 16

1. Preheat oven to 250F (120C). Line 2 baking sheets with parchment paper.
2. In a mixer bowl, beat egg whites with an electric mixer at high speed until soft peaks form. Gradually beat in sugar; beat until stiff and glossy. Fold in nuts.
3. Spoon 16 oval shapes of meringue onto paper-lined baking sheets. Bake in preheated oven 2 hours or until dry. When done, meringues will lift easily from paper. Remove from paper; cool on a wire rack.
4. In a medium bowl, whip cream until stiff peaks form. Fold in coffee mixture. Spread coffee cream on half of meringues; top with remaining meringues. Decorate with chocolate curls. Makes 8 servings.

Baked Stuffed Peaches

1 cup sponge-cake crumbs
3/4 cup almonds, finely ground
Grated peel and juice of 1 medium orange
4 large ripe peaches or nectarines, halved
2 tablespoons sugar
2 tablespoons butter or margarine
1/2 cup sweet white wine

1. Preheat oven to 350F (175C). Butter a baking dish large enough to hold peach or nectarine halves in 1 layer.
2. In a medium bowl, blend cake crumbs, almonds, orange peel and orange juice into a paste.
3. Spoon some almond mixture on top of each peach half. Or, fill a pastry bag fitted with an open star tip with almond mixture. Pipe mixture over peach or nectarine halves.
4. Place filled peaches or nectarines in buttered baking dish in a single layer. Sprinkle with sugar; dot with butter or margarine.
5. Pour wine around fruit; bake in preheated oven 15 to 20 minutes or until fruit is almost tender and topping is lightly browned. Serve immediately. Makes 4 servings.

Kiwifruit Pavlova

4 egg whites
1-1/4 cups sugar
1 teaspoon vanilla extract
1 teaspoon lemon juice
2 teaspoons cornstarch
1 pint whipping cream (2 cups), whipped
6 kiwifruit, peeled, sliced

This classic dessert from Australia is similar to a meringue. However, cornstarch, lemon juice and vanilla extract are added to the beaten egg whites. The additional ingredients and the shorter cooking time produce a crisp exterior and a soft chewy center.

1. Preheat oven to 300F (150C). Line a baking sheet with parchment paper. Draw a 9-inch circle on parchment paper.
2. In a large bowl, beat egg whites until stiff but not dry. Gradually beat in sugar, 1 tablespoon at a time. Beat until mixture is thick and glossy.
3. Fold in vanilla, lemon juice and cornstarch. Spoon mixture inside circle on parchment paper. Hollow center; make outside edge slightly higher.
4. Bake in preheated oven 1 hour. Cool on a wire rack. Remove paper. Place meringue on a flat serving plate.
5. Fill center with whipped cream. Top cream with kiwifruit slices. Makes 8 servings.

Variation
Substitute other fresh fruits for kiwifruit. Try a combination of strawberry, pineapple and mango or canned or fresh lychees, decorated with tiny mint leaves.

Clockwise from top: Kiwifruit Pavlova, Coffee-Cream & Meringue Sandwiches, Baked Stuffed Peaches

Crepes Suzette

Crepes:
1/2 cup all-purpose flour
2 tablespoons sugar
2 eggs
2/3 cup milk
2 tablespoons butter or margarine, melted
2 tablespoons cognac, if desired
Butter or margarine for cooking

Orange Butter:
1/2 cup butter or margarine
1/3 cup sugar
Grated peel and juice of 1 large orange
1/4 cup orange-flavored liqueur
1 tablespoon brandy

1. Sift flour and sugar into a medium bowl. In a small bowl, beat eggs and milk until blended. Gradually stir into flour mixture; beat until smooth. Beat in melted butter or margarine. Stir in cognac, if desired.
2. Pour batter into a pitcher. Cover and refrigerate 1 hour.
3. Melt about 1 teaspoon butter or margarine in a 6- or 7-inch crepe pan or skillet. Stir batter; pour about 2 tablespoons batter into crepe pan. Swirl pan so batter makes a thin layer in bottom of pan. Cook over medium heat 1 to 1-1/2 minutes or until small bubbles begin to form on surface of crepe.
4. Turn crepe over; cook 1 to 1-1/2 minutes or until bottom is golden brown. Slide crepe onto a flat plate. Repeat with remaining batter, making 12 crepes.
5. To make Orange Butter, melt butter or margarine in a medium saucepan. Stir in sugar, orange peel and orange juice until blended. Cook until sugar dissolves.
6. Fold crepes in quarters. Pour warm Orange Butter into a chafing dish or shallow flameproof serving dish. Arrange folded crepes in dish; spoon Orange Butter over crepes.
7. Heat liqueur and brandy in a small pan over low heat. Pour warmed liqueur and brandy over crepes; ignite carefully. Shake pan until flames die. Serve immediately. Makes 6 servings.

Orange Cake with Rum-&-Raisin Filling

Cake:
5 eggs, separated
3/4 cup sugar
1 tablespoon grated orange peel
1 tablespoon orange juice
1 tablespoon dark rum
1 cup cake flour
1/2 cup ground almonds
1/2 teaspoon salt

Filling:
1/3 cup raisins
3 tablespoons dark rum
1/2 pint whipping cream (1 cup)
2 tablespoons powdered sugar

To decorate:
Powdered sugar
Orange sections

1. Preheat oven to 350F (175C). Grease and flour an 8-inch springform pan. To make cake, in a large bowl, beat egg yolks and sugar until thick and lemon-colored. Stir in orange peel, orange juice and rum. Fold in flour, ground almonds and salt.
2. In a medium bowl, beat egg whites until stiff but not dry. Fold beaten egg whites into batter.
3. Pour mixture into prepared pan. Bake in preheated oven 40 to 45 minutes or until a wooden pick inserted in center comes out clean. Cool cake in pan on a wire rack 10 minutes. Remove from pan; cool completely on wire rack. Cut cake into 2 layers.
4. To make filling, chop raisins; place in a small bowl. Stir in rum; set aside.
5. In a medium bowl, whip cream until soft peaks form. Beat in powdered sugar; beat until stiff peaks form. Spoon 3/4 cup whipped cream into a pastry bag fitted with an open star tip; refrigerate. Fold raisin-and-rum mixture into remaining whipped cream.
6. Place 1 cake layer on a serving plate, cut-side down; spread raisin mixture on top. Cover with remaining cake layer, cut-side down. Dust with powdered sugar. Pipe reserved whipped cream on top of cake; decorate with orange sections. Refrigerate until served. Makes 8 servings.

Traditional Baked Cheesecake

Crust:
1-1/4 cups graham-cracker crumbs
2 tablespoons sugar
1/4 cup butter or margarine, melted

Cheese Filling:
4 (8-oz.) pkgs. cream cheese, room temperature
1 cup sugar
2 eggs
1/4 cup all-purpose flour
Grated peel of 1 lemon
1 cup dairy sour cream

To decorate:
Fresh strawberries or other fruit

1. Preheat oven to 350F (175C). Grease a 9-inch springform pan. To make crust, in a small bowl, combine cracker crumbs and sugar. Stir in butter or margarine. Press crumbs onto bottom of greased pan. Bake 10 minutes. Remove from oven; cool on a wire rack. Increase oven temperature to 400F (205C).
2. To make filling, in a large bowl, beat cream cheese and sugar until smooth. Beat in eggs, flour and lemon peel until blended. Stir in sour cream. Pour cheese mixture over bottom crust; smooth top.
3. Bake in preheated oven 45 to 50 minutes or until center is set. Turn off oven; leave cheesecake in oven, with oven door slightly ajar, 3 hours. Remove from oven; cool completely in pan on a wire rack. Refrigerate until served.
4. To serve, run tip of a knife around inside edge of pan. Release and remove pan side. Place cheesecake on a serving plate. Decorate top of cake with strawberries or other fruit. Makes 12 to 14 servings.

Top to bottom: Traditional Baked Cheesecake, Orange Cake with Rum-&-Raisin Filling

Baked Desserts

Bread & Butter Pudding

2 tablespoons butter or margarine, room temperature
4 slices day-old white bread, crusts removed
1/4 cup apricot jam
1/2 cup raisins
2 eggs
2 tablespoons sugar
2 cups milk
Ground cinnamon

---

1. Butter a shallow 1-1/2-quart casserole. Spread butter or margarine on bread. Spread each buttered slice with apricot jam; cut bread diagonally into 4 triangles.
2. Arrange 1/2 the triangles in bottom of buttered casserole; sprinkle with 1/2 the raisins. Top with remaining triangles and raisins.
3. In a medium bowl, beat eggs, sugar and milk until blended. Pour over bread and raisins; let stand at room temperature 1 hour.
4. Preheat oven to 350F (175C). Place casserole in a roasting pan. Add enough boiling water to come halfway up sides of casserole.
5. Bake 50 to 60 minutes or until a knife tip inserted slightly off center comes out clean. Remove from roasting pan; cool on a wire rack 5 to 10 minutes.
6. Sprinkle with cinnamon; serve warm. Makes 4 to 6 servings.

Baked Pears in White Wine

6 tablespoons orange marmalade
6 tablespoons coarsely crushed macaroons
6 large ripe pears, peeled, halved, cored
1 cup sweet white wine
3 tablespoons butter or margarine

---

1. Preheat oven to 350F (175C). Grease a shallow oven-proof dish large enough to hold pears in a single layer.
2. In a small bowl, blend marmalade and macaroons. Place pear halves in greased dish, cut-side up. Fill pears with marmalade mixture.
3. Pour wine around pears. Dot filled pears with butter or margarine.
4. Bake in preheated oven 20 to 30 minutes or until tender when tested with a wooden pick.
5. Serve warm or at room temperature. Makes 6 servings.

Spiced Bread Pudding

8 slices day-old whole-wheat bread, crumbled
1-3/4 cups milk
1/4 cup butter or margarine
1/4 cup firmly packed dark-brown sugar
1/3 cup raisins
1/3 cup currants
1 teaspoon ground cinnamon
1 teaspoon ground ginger
1/2 teaspoon ground nutmeg
2 eggs, beaten
Dark-brown sugar

---

1. Preheat oven to 350F (175C). Grease an 11" x 7" baking dish.
2. Place bread in a medium bowl; set aside. In a small saucepan, combine milk, butter or margarine and 1/4 cup brown sugar. Stir over medium heat until mixture comes to a boil and butter or margarine melts.
3. Stir hot milk mixture into bread. Let stand 15 minutes, stirring occasionally. Stir in raisins, currants, cinnamon, ginger, nutmeg and eggs. Pour into greased dish.
4. Bake 40 to 45 minutes or until a knife tip inserted slightly off center comes out clean. Sprinkle with brown sugar while still hot.
5. Cut into squares; serve immediately. Makes 6 to 8 servings.

Clockwise from top left: Spiced Bread Pudding, Bread & Butter Pudding, Baked Pears in White Wine

Harvest Apple Pie

Double recipe Pastry, page 43

6 to 7 medium, tart apples, peeled, sliced
1 tablespoon lemon juice
4 teaspoons cornstarch
1 teaspoon grated lemon peel
1 teaspoon ground cinnamon
1/4 teaspoon ground nutmeg
1/4 teaspoon ground allspice
1/2 to 3/4 cup sugar
2 tablespoons butter or margarine, diced
Milk
Sugar

To serve:
Sharp Cheddar cheese

1. Preheat oven to 425F (220C). Make pastry as directed in step 2. On a lightly floured surface, roll out 1/2 of pastry to a 12-inch circle. Use to line a 9- or 10-inch pie pan. Do not trim pastry edge.
2. Place apples in a large bowl; sprinkle with lemon juice. In a small bowl, combine cornstarch, lemon peel, cinnamon, nutmeg and allspice. Add sugar to taste, depending on tartness of apples. Sprinkle sugar mixture over apples; toss to coat.
3. Arrange apple slices in pastry-lined pan, mounding apples in center. Dot with butter or margarine.
4. On a lightly floured surface, roll out remaining pastry to an 11- or 12-inch circle. Carefully place pastry over apples. Trim pastry edges to 1 inch beyond rim of pie pan. Fold overhang under to build up edge; press edges together to seal. Pinch folded edge up to form high edge; flute.
5. Cut 3 or 4 slits in center of top crust to allow steam to escape. Brush crust with milk; sprinkle with sugar.
6. Bake in preheated oven 45 to 50 minutes or until crust is golden and apples are tender. Cool on a wire rack.
7. Serve warm or cold with cheese. Makes 6 to 8 servings.

Banana Puffs with Walnut-Rum Sauce

1/2 (17-1/2-oz.) pkg. frozen puff pastry, thawed
4 medium, firm-ripe bananas, peeled
1 egg white, slightly beaten
1 tablespoon sugar

Walnut-Rum Sauce:
2/3 cup water
1/3 cup packed light-brown sugar
1/4 cup butter or margarine
1/4 cup chopped walnuts
2 tablespoons dark rum

1. Cut pastry into 4 pieces. On a lightly floured surface, roll out each piece until large enough to cover a banana.
2. Wrap bananas in pastry. Brush edges with water; seal. Cut away excess pastry; reserve.
3. Roll trimmings from each banana-filled pastry to a narrow 10-inch strip. Wrap a pastry strip around each pastry; form into a bow.
4. Rinse a baking sheet with water. Place pastries on damp baking sheet. Brush with egg white; sprinkle with sugar. Bake in a preheated oven 20 to 25 minutes or until puffed and golden.
5. To make sauce, in a medium saucepan over low heat, combine water and brown sugar. Stir until sugar dissolves. Boil rapidly about 5 minutes or until slightly syrupy. Remove from heat; stir in remaining ingredients. Stir until butter or margarine melts.
6. Serve sauce immediately with warm banana puffs. Makes 4 servings.

Layered Apple Bake

1 lb. cooking apples, peeled, cored, sliced (4 medium)
Grated peel and juice of 1/2 lemon
3/4 cup sugar
1 egg, beaten
1/2 cup butter or margarine
4 cups fresh white-bread crumbs

To serve:
Vanilla ice cream

1. In a medium saucepan, combine apples, lemon peel and lemon juice. Simmer until soft. Stir in 1/2 cup sugar. Cool slightly; beat in egg and 2 tablespoons butter or margarine. Cool.
2. Preheat oven to 425F (220C). In a medium skillet, melt remaining butter or margarine. Stir in bread crumbs and remaining sugar.
3. Press 1/2 the crumb mixture on bottom of a 9-inch oven-proof dish. Spread apple mixture over crumbs; top with remaining crumb mixture. Press down gently.
4. Bake in preheated oven 30 minutes. Cool on a wire rack 5 minutes; turn out on a serving plate.
5. Serve warm with vanilla ice cream. Makes 6 servings.

Plum Dumplings

8 firm red plums
8 teaspoons sugar
Pastry, page 43
Milk
Sugar

To serve:
Whipped cream

1. Split each plum enough to remove and discard pits; remove pits. Fill cavity with 1 teaspoon sugar; set plums aside. Grease a baking sheet.

2. Preheat oven to 400F (205C). Make pastry as directed in step 2, page 43. Divide pastry into 8 pieces.

3. On a lightly floured surface, roll out each pastry piece into a square large enough to cover a plum. Place a sugar-filled plum in center of each pastry square. Draw corners of pastry to center, see photo. Trim off excess pastry. Brush edges with water; seal.

4. On a lightly floured surface, roll out pastry trimmings; cut out pastry leaves. Decorate each dumpling with pastry leaves made from trimmings.

5. Place dumplings on greased baking sheet. Brush with milk; sprinkle with sugar.

6. Bake in preheated oven 20 to 25 minutes or until crisp and golden on outside and tender in center when pierced with a wooden pick.

7. Serve immediately with whipped cream. Makes 4 servings.

Clockwise from top left: Custard Sauce, page 28; Plum Dumplings; Banana Puffs with Walnut-Rum Sauce

Almond & Pear Crepes

8 Crepes, page 54

Filling:
1 (16-oz.) can sliced pears
1/2 cup butter or margarine, room temperature
1/2 cup powdered sugar, sifted
1/3 cup finely ground blanched almonds

1. Prepare crepes according to recipe on page 54. Place small sheets of waxed paper between extra crepes; wrap in foil. Freeze for another use.
2. Drain pears, reserving syrup. Coarsely chop pears; set aside.
3. In a small bowl, beat butter or margarine and powdered sugar until light and fluffy. Fold in almonds and chopped pears.
4. Preheat broiler. Grease a shallow, flameproof baking dish. Fold each crepe in quarters. Spoon a little pear filling into 1 quarter of each crepe. Place filled crepes in a single layer in greased dish. Spoon a little reserved pear syrup over each crepe.
5. Place dish under preheated broiler, 3 to 4 inches from source of heat; broil 3 to 4 minutes or until crepes are lightly browned.
6. Serve immediately. Makes 4 servings.

Left to right: Almond & Pear Crepes, Raspberry Clafoutis

Raspberry Clafoutis

3 eggs
1/4 cup granulated sugar
1/2 cup sifted all-purpose flour
Pinch salt
1-1/4 cups milk
3 tablespoons butter or margarine, melted
1 (10-oz.) pkg. frozen raspberries, thawed, drained
Superfine sugar

Clafoutis, a thick fruit pancake, is baked in the oven and served warm. It originates from the Limousin area in France. It is traditionally made with black cherries.

1. Preheat oven to 400F (205C). Grease a 9-inch au gratin dish.
2. In a medium bowl, beat eggs and sugar 5 minutes or until pale and foamy. Fold in flour and salt. Stir in milk and butter or margarine to make a smooth batter.
3. Pour 1/2 of batter into prepared dish. Bake 15 minutes.
4. Arrange raspberries on baked batter; carefully pour remaining batter around fruit.
5. Bake 35 minutes longer or until top is golden.
6. Sprinkle with superfine sugar; serve immediately. Makes 4 to 6 servings.

Strawberry-&-Cream-Filled Crepes

Crepes, page 54
1 pint fresh strawberries, washed, hulled
1/2 pint whipping cream (1 cup)
2 tablespoons powdered sugar
1 teaspoon vanilla extract
1/2 cup strawberry jam

1. Make crepes according to recipe, page 54. Keep crepes warm in a low oven.
2. Slice 6 to 8 strawberries; reserve for decoration. Coarsely chop remaining strawberries; set aside.
3. In a medium bowl, whip cream until soft peaks form. Add powdered sugar and vanilla; beat until stiff peaks form. Fold chopped strawberries into whipped-cream mixture.
4. Spread each crepe with 1 to 2 teaspoons strawberry jam. Spoon a heaping tablespoon strawberry cream down center of each crepe; fold sides over filling.
5. Place 2 crepes, seam-side down, on dessert plates. Top with remaining strawberry cream and sliced strawberries. Serve filled crepes immediately. Makes 6 servings.

Apricot & Almond Pudding

1 (16-oz.) can apricot halves, well drained
6 tablespoons butter or margarine, room temperature
1/2 cup sugar
2 eggs
1/2 teaspoon almond extract
1 cup sifted all-purpose flour
1-1/2 teaspoons baking powder
1/3 cup ground blanched almonds
1/4 cup milk
6 whole blanched almonds

1. Grease a 1-quart heatproof bowl or pudding mold. Reserve 6 apricot halves. Chop remaining apricots.
2. In a medium bowl, beat butter or margarine and sugar until light and fluffy. Beat in eggs and almond extract until blended.
3. In a small bowl, combine flour, baking powder and ground almonds; fold into butter mixture. Stir in milk until blended; fold in chopped apricots.
4. Place 1 almond in cavity of each reserved apricot half. Arrange apricots, cut-side down, in bottom of greased bowl or mold. Spoon batter carefully over apricots. Cover with a double thickness of greased waxed paper. Wrap in foil; secure with kitchen string.
5. Place bowl on a trivet in a large saucepan. Add enough boiling water to come 3/4 up side of bowl or mold. Cover; steam 2 hours, adding boiling water as necessary. Remove pudding from saucepan. Cool slightly.
6. To serve, unwrap; invert pudding on a serving plate. Remove mold or bowl. Serve warm. Makes 6 servings.

Left to right: Apricot & Almond Pudding, Almond & Fig Pudding

Raisin-Bread Pudding

2-1/2 cups milk
1/2 cup sugar
3 tablespoons butter or margarine
3 eggs, slightly beaten
1 teaspoon vanilla extract
12 slices raisin bread
1/3 cup raisins
1 teaspoon ground cinnamon
1/4 teaspoon ground nutmeg
To serve:
Custard Sauce, page 28

1. Preheat oven to 350F (175C). Lightly grease a 1-1/2-quart casserole. In a medium saucepan, combine milk, sugar and butter or margarine. Cook over low heat until butter or margarine melts, sugar dissolves and tiny bubbles form around edge of pan. Remove from heat.
2. Stir 1/4 cup hot milk mixture into eggs until well blended. Return mixture to saucepan, stirring until thoroughly blended. Stir in vanilla.
3. Remove crusts from bread, if desired. Cut bread into small cubes. In a medium bowl, combine bread cubes, raisins, cinnamon and nutmeg. Stir milk mixture into bread mixture. Spoon into greased casserole. Place casserole in a roasting pan; add enough boiling water to come halfway up side of casserole.
4. Bake 50 to 60 minutes or until tip of a knife inserted slightly off center comes out clean. Remove from roasting pan; cool on a wire rack 5 to 10 minutes.
5. Serve warm or at room temperature with custard sauce. Makes 4 to 6 servings.

Apple Crisp

6 medium, tart apples, peeled, cored, sliced
2 tablespoons lemon juice
1/4 cup sugar
Topping:
1/2 cup all-purpose flour
1/2 cup regular rolled oats
1/2 cup firmly packed brown sugar
1/4 cup granulated sugar
1 teaspoon ground cinnamon
1/4 teaspoon ground nutmeg
6 tablespoons butter or margarine
To serve:
Ice cream or sweetened whipped cream

1. Preheat oven to 375F (190C).
2. Place apples in a large bowl; sprinkle with lemon juice and sugar. Toss to coat. Arrange apples in an ungreased deep 9-inch pie plate or 2-quart casserole.
3. To make topping, in a medium bowl, combine flour, oats, brown sugar, granulated sugar, cinnamon and nutmeg. With a pastry blender or 2 knives, cut in butter or margarine until mixture resembles coarse crumbs. Sprinkle crumbs over apples.
4. Bake 25 to 30 minutes or until apples are tender and topping is lightly browned. Cool on a wire rack 5 to 10 minutes.
5. Serve warm with ice cream or sweetened whipped cream. Makes 4 to 6 servings.

Almond & Fig Pudding

1/2 cup butter or margarine, room temperature
1/3 cup sugar
2 eggs
1 tablespoon grated lemon peel
1 cup sifted all-purpose flour
1-1/2 teaspoons baking powder
1/3 cup milk
1/2 (7-oz.) pkg. marzipan, diced
1 (17-oz.) can figs, drained, cut in half

1. Grease a 1-quart heatproof bowl or pudding mold. In a medium bowl, beat butter or margarine and sugar until light and fluffy. Beat in eggs and lemon peel until blended. In a small bowl, blend flour and baking powder; fold into sugar mixture. Stir in milk until blended. Stir in marzipan.
2. Place 6 fig halves, cut-side down, in bottom of greased bowl or mold. Spoon 1/2 the batter over figs. Top with remaining figs; spoon remaining batter over figs.
3. Cover with a double thickness of greased waxed paper. Wrap in foil; secure with kitchen string. Place bowl or mold on a trivet in a large saucepan. Add enough boiling water to come 3/4 up side of mold or bowl. Cover; steam 2 hours, adding boiling water as necessary. Remove pudding from saucepan. Cool slightly.
4. To serve, unwrap; invert pudding on a serving plate. Remove mold or bowl. Serve warm. Makes 6 servings.

Indian Pudding

1/2 cup yellow cornmeal
1 qt. milk (4 cups)
1/2 cup molasses
1/4 cup firmly packed brown sugar
3 tablespoons butter or margarine
1 teaspoon ground cinnamon
1/2 teaspoon ground ginger
1/2 teaspoon salt
2 eggs
1/2 cup chopped almonds

1. Preheat oven to 350F (175C). Grease a 1-quart casserole or baking dish. Place cornmeal in top of double boiler. In a medium saucepan, scald 3 cups milk. Pour scalded milk over cornmeal, stirring constantly.
2. Cook over pan of simmering water about 20 minutes, stirring constantly. Stir in molasses, brown sugar, butter or margarine, cinnamon, ginger and salt until blended. Cook 5 minutes, stirring constantly. Set aside.
3. In a medium bowl, beat eggs with remaining 1 cup milk until blended. Stir into cornmeal mixture.
4. Pour mixture into greased casserole. Place casserole in a roasting pan. Add enough boiling water to come halfway up side of casserole.
5. Bake 60 to 70 minutes or until tip of a knife inserted slightly off center comes out clean. Remove from roasting pan; cool on a wire rack 5 minutes.
6. Sprinkle with almonds; serve warm. Makes 6 servings.

Christmas Pudding

3/4 cup dark raisins
3/4 cup golden raisins
3/4 cup currants
1/2 cup finely chopped mixed candied fruit
1/4 cup finely chopped red candied cherries
Grated peel and juice of 1 orange
3/4 cup dark beer or ale
1-1/4 cups all-purpose flour
1 teaspoon baking powder
1 teaspoon ground cinnamon
1/2 teaspoon ground nutmeg
1/4 teaspoon ground cloves
2 cups fresh bread crumbs
1 cup firmly packed brown sugar
3/4 cup shredded suet
1 tart apple, peeled, cored, grated
1 carrot, grated
1/2 cup chopped toasted blanched almonds
3 eggs
2 tablespoons molasses

To serve:
1/4 cup brandy, cognac or dark rum, if desired

1. In a medium bowl, combine raisins, currants, mixed candied fruit, candied cherries and orange peel. Stir in beer or ale; let stand 30 minutes.
2. Grease 2 (1-quart) pudding molds or heatproof bowls.
3. In a large bowl, combine flour, baking powder, cinnamon, nutmeg and cloves. With a wooden spoon, stir in bread crumbs, brown sugar, suet, apple, carrot and almonds until blended. In a small bowl, blend eggs, orange juice and molasses. Stir egg mixture and fruit mixture into dry ingredients. Stir until blended.
4. Divide mixture equally between greased molds or bowls. Cover with a double thickness of greased waxed paper. Wrap in foil; secure with kitchen string. Place covered molds or bowls on a rack in a large kettle. Add enough boiling water to come 3/4 up side of molds or bowls. Cover; steam 4 hours, adding more boiling water as necessary.
5. Remove molds or bowls; cool covered puddings completely on a wire rack. Recover molds with clean waxed paper and foil. Store in a cool place until ready to serve.
6. To serve, steam puddings as directed above about 1 hour. Cool slightly; uncover puddings. Invert on serving plates; remove molds or bowls.
7. If desired, warm brandy in a small saucepan; pour over pudding. Carefully ignite brandy; serve while flaming. Makes 12 to 14 servings.

Peach Cobbler

1/3 cup sugar
1 tablespoon cornstarch
1/2 teaspoon ground cinnamon
5 to 6 medium peaches, peeled
     sliced (about 2 lb.)
1 tablespoon lemon juice

Topping:
1 cup all-purpose flour
2 tablespoons sugar
1-1/2 teaspoons baking powder
1/2 teaspoon salt
1/4 cup butter or margarine
1/2 cup milk
Ground cinnamon

1. Preheat oven to 400F (205C). In a large saucepan, combine sugar, cornstarch and cinnamon. Stir in peaches and lemon juice until coated. Cook over low heat until mixture comes to a boil and thickens, stirring gently. Pour peach mixture into an ungreased 2-quart casserole.
2. To make topping, in a medium bowl, combine flour, sugar, baking powder and salt. With a pastry blender or 2 knives, cut in butter or margarine until mixture resembles coarse crumbs. Stir in milk until blended.
3. Drop dough by heaping tablespoons on top of hot peach mixture, making 6 mounds of dough. Sprinkle cinnamon over dough. Bake 25 to 30 minutes or until topping is lightly browned.
4. Serve warm. Makes 6 servings.

Holly leaves and berries are poisonous; do not eat.

Christmas Tart

Pastry, page 38
6 tablespoons butter or margarine
2 eggs, slightly beaten
1/4 cup sugar
2/3 cup chopped mixed candied fruit

1. Preheat oven to 350F (175C). Make pastry through step 1. On a lightly floured surface, roll out pastry to an 11-inch circle. Use to line a 9-inch quiche pan or flan pan with removable bottom. Pastry should come only halfway up side of pan.
2. To make filling, in a small saucepan, combine butter or margarine, eggs and sugar. Cook over medium heat until mixture comes to a boil, stirring constantly. Remove from heat immediately; stir in candied fruit. Pour mixture into pastry-lined pan; smooth top.
3. Bake 30 to 35 minutes or until center is set and pastry is golden brown. Cool in pan on a wire rack.
4. Makes 6 servings.

Clockwise from left: Sweet Noodle Pudding, Christmas Tart, Upside-Down Plum Pie

Lemon Sponge Pudding

1/4 cup butter or margarine, room temperature
1/2 cup sugar
3 eggs, separated
1/4 cup all-purpose flour, sifted
Grated peel and juice of 1 lemon
3/4 cup milk

1. Preheat oven to 350F (175C). Grease a 1-1/2-quart casserole. In a medium bowl, beat butter or margarine and sugar until light and fluffy. Beat in egg yolks, 1 at a time, beating well after each addition.
2. Fold in flour, lemon peel and lemon juice. Beat in milk until blended. In a medium bowl, beat egg whites until stiff peaks form. Fold into batter. Pour mixture into greased casserole; smooth top. Place casserole in a roasting pan; add enough boiling water to come halfway up side of casserole.
3. Bake 35 to 40 minutes or until top is golden brown. Remove from roasting pan; cool on a wire rack 5 minutes.
4. Serve warm or at room temperature. Makes 4 to 6 servings.

Sweet Noodle Pudding

3 cups medium egg noodles (4 oz.)
1/4 cup butter or margarine, melted
2 eggs, separated
1/2 cup plus 2 tablespoons sugar
1 teaspoon vanilla extract
1/2 cup dairy sour cream
1/2 cup small-curd cottage cheese
1 cup milk
1/2 teaspoon ground cinnamon

1. Preheat oven to 375F (190C). Grease a 1-1/2-quart baking dish.
2. In a large saucepan, cook noodles according to package directions until almost tender. Drain well; place in greased baking dish. Stir in butter or margarine.
3. In a medium bowl, beat egg yolks, 1/2 cup sugar, vanilla, sour cream and cottage cheese until smooth and blended. Gradually stir in milk.
4. In a medium bowl, beat egg whites until stiff but not dry. Fold beaten egg whites into cheese mixture. Pour cheese mixture over noodles; stir gently. In a small bowl, combine remaining 2 tablespoons sugar and cinnamon; sprinkle over noodles.
5. Bake 40 to 45 minutes or until center is set.
6. Serve warm. Makes 4 to 6 servings.

Upside-Down Plum Pie

1-1/4 cups all-purpose flour
1/3 cup ground almonds
1/2 cup sugar
1/2 cup plus 2 tablespoons butter or margarine
1 egg yolk
1 to 2 tablespoons iced water
6 to 7 small red plums, halved, pitted (about 1-1/4 lb.)

1. In a medium bowl, combine flour, almonds and 1/4 cup sugar. With a pastry blender or 2 knives, cut in 1/2 cup butter or margarine until mixture resembles coarse crumbs.
2. In a small bowl, blend egg yolk with 1 tablespoon water; sprinkle over flour mixture. Toss with a fork until mixture holds together. Add remaining water, if necessary. Shape into a ball; wrap in plastic wrap. Refrigerate 30 minutes.
3. Preheat oven to 375F (190C). Melt remaining 2 tablespoons butter or margarine in a pie pan in preheated oven. Stir in remaining 1/4 cup sugar; cook until sugar dissolves and syrup is caramel in color. Remove from heat. Place plums, cut-side up, in bottom of pie pan.
4. On a lightly floured surface, roll out dough to a 10-inch circle. Place over plums, tucking edges in around edge of pan.
5. Bake 35 to 45 minutes or until pastry is golden brown. Cool in pan on a wire rack 5 minutes.
6. Invert onto a serving plate; serve warm. Makes 6 to 8 servings.

Prune & Almond Custard

1 cup pitted prunes
Water
About 20 whole almonds
3 eggs, separated
1/2 cup sugar
2/3 cup whipping cream
2/3 cup half and half
1/4 cup butter or margarine
1 tablespoon port
Few drops of almond extract

This dessert is interesting because of the contrast in flavors and textures. The top is a puffy meringue, the middle is a smooth custard and the bottom layer is the prunes and crunchy almonds. Meringue top will collapse when chilled.

1. Place prunes in a medium saucepan; cover with water. Simmer 10 minutes or until tender. Cool in cooking liquid. Drain and discard cooking liquid. Place an almond in center of each prune. Grease a 1-1/2-quart casserole.
2. Preheat oven to 350F (175C). Arrange stuffed prunes in a single layer in greased casserole.
3. In a medium bowl, beat egg yolks and sugar until thick and pale. In a medium saucepan, heat whipping cream, half and half and butter or margarine until butter or margarine melts. Beat hot cream mixture into egg mixture. Stir in port and almond extract.
4. Beat egg whites until stiff but not dry. Fold beaten egg whites into egg mixture.
5. Pour egg mixture over prunes. Place casserole in a roasting pan. Add enough boiling water to come halfway up side of casserole.
6. Bake in preheated oven about 1 hour. After 30 minutes, if top is getting too brown, reduce oven temperature to 325F (165C).
7. Serve at room temperature or refrigerate until chilled. Makes 4 servings.

Steamed Chocolate Pudding

1/2 cup butter or margarine, room temperature
1 cup sugar
2 eggs
1-1/3 cups all-purpose flour
1/3 cup unsweetened cocoa powder
1-1/2 teaspoons baking powder
1/3 cup milk

Chocolate Sauce:
3 oz. semisweet chocolate, broken into pieces
1/4 cup light corn syrup
2 tablespoons butter or margarine
2 tablespoons water
1/2 teaspoon vanilla extract

1. Grease a 1-1/2-quart pudding mold or heatproof bowl. In a medium bowl, beat butter or margarine and sugar until light and fluffy. Beat in eggs, 1 at a time, beating well after each addition. Sift flour, cocoa powder and baking powder over creamed mixture; fold in. Stir in milk until well blended.
2. Spoon into greased mold or bowl. Cover with a double thickness of greased waxed paper. Wrap in foil; secure with kitchen string.
3. Place covered pudding on a trivet in a large saucepan. Add enough boiling water to come halfway up side of mold or bowl. Cover; steam 1-1/2 hours, adding more boiling water as necessary.
4. Remove mold; cool covered pudding on a wire rack 5 minutes. Uncover; invert on a serving plate. Remove mold or bowl.
5. To make Chocolate Sauce, in a medium saucepan, combine chocolate, corn syrup and butter or margarine. Cook over low heat until chocolate melts, stirring constantly. Stir in water and vanilla until blended. Pour sauce over pudding; serve immediately. Makes 6 to 8 servings.

Left to right: Upside-Down Toffee-Apple Pie, Pineapple Upside-Down Cake

Upside-Down Toffee-Apple Pie

1-3/4 cups all-purpose flour
2 teaspoons baking powder
1 teaspoon salt
3/4 cup vegetable shortening
5 to 6 tablespoons water
1/4 cup butter or margarine
2/3 cup firmly packed brown sugar
3 or 4 medium, tart apples, peeled, cored,
    thinly sliced (1-1/2 lb.)

1. Sift flour, baking powder and salt into a medium bowl. With a pastry blender or 2 knives, cut in shortening. Add 5 tablespoons water; stir to make a stiff dough. Add remaining water, if necessary. Cover; refrigerate 1 hour.
2. Preheat oven to 350F (175C). In a small bowl, blend butter or margarine and 1/3 cup brown sugar. Spread over bottom and up side of a 9-inch pie pan.
3. Divide pastry in half. On a lightly floured surface, roll out 1/2 of pastry; place in prepared pie pan. Do not trim pastry edges. Arrange 1/2 of apples in pastry-lined pan. Sprinkle apples with remaining 1/3 cup brown sugar. Top with remaining apples. Fold pastry edges in towards center.
4. On a lightly floured surface, roll out remaining pastry. Brush pastry with water; place over apples, brushed-side down. Tuck in edges.
5. Bake in preheated oven 60 to 65 minutes or until pastry is golden and apples are tender. Cool on a wire rack 5 minutes.
6. Invert on a serving plate; remove pan. Serve immediately. Makes 8 servings.

Pineapple Upside-Down Cake

1/4 cup butter or margarine
1/2 cup firmly packed brown sugar
6 slices canned pineapple, well drained
6 candied or maraschino cherries
1-1/4 cups all-purpose flour
1 cup granulated sugar
2 teaspoons baking powder
1/2 teaspoon salt
1 egg
6 tablespoons vegetable shortening
3/4 cup milk
1 teaspoon vanilla extract

To serve:
Sweetened whipped cream, if desired

1. Preheat oven to 350F (175C). Place butter or margarine in a 9-inch cake pan. Place pan in oven until butter or margarine melts. Stir brown sugar into melted butter or margarine.
2. Arrange pineapple slices in a single layer in butter-sugar mixture. Place 1 cherry, cut-side up, in center of each pineapple slice.
3. To make cake, sift flour, granulated sugar, baking powder and salt into a large mixer bowl. Add egg, shortening, milk and vanilla; beat at low speed until blended. Increase speed to high; beat 3 minutes. Pour batter evenly over pineapple slices; smooth top.
4. Bake 40 to 45 minutes or until a wooden pick inserted in center of cake comes out clean. Cool in pan on a wire rack 2 minutes. Invert cake on a serving plate; leave pan over cake 3 to 4 minutes. Carefully remove pan.
5. Serve warm or cold with sweetened whipped cream, if desired. Makes 6 servings.

Frozen Desserts

Frozen Zabaglione

6 egg yolks
6 tablespoons sugar
6 tablespoons Marsala
2/3 cup whipping cream

To decorate:
Whipped cream
Toasted nuts or angelica leaves

---

1. In a large heatproof bowl, combine egg yolks, sugar and Marsala. Place over a pan of simmering water; beat 10 minutes or until thick and pale.
2. Remove from heat; beat 5 minutes or until cool.
3. In a small bowl, whip cream until soft peaks form. Fold whipped cream into cooled egg mixture.
4. Spoon mixture into an ice-cream container. Freeze in an ice-cream maker according to manufacturer's directions. Decorate with whipped cream, nuts or angelica leaves.
5. For special occasions, make lemon baskets as illustrated. Fill with softened zabaglione. Place in freezer until firm. Makes 6 to 8 servings.

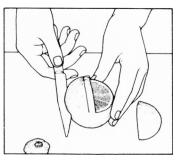
1/Using a sharp knife, form a handle.

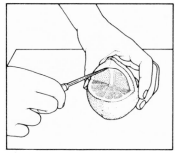
2/Remove pulp, leaving pith and peel intact.

Lemon Ice Cream

Grated peel of 2 lemons
Juice of 3 lemons
3/4 cup sugar
1-1/4 cups whipping cream
1 cup milk

To decorate:
Angelica leaves, if desired

---

1. In a medium bowl, combine lemon peel, lemon juice and sugar. Add cream; whip until soft peaks form.
2. Slowly beat in milk. Pour into an ice-cream container. Freeze in an ice-cream maker according to manufacturer's directions.
3. Serve ice cream in dessert dishes. Decorate with angelica leaves, if desired. Makes 8 servings.

Strawberry Ice

1/2 cup sugar
1 cup water
1-1/2 teaspoons lemon juice
2 cups fresh or frozen strawberries, pureed

---

1. In a medium saucepan, combine sugar and water. Stir over low heat until sugar dissolves. Boil 3 minutes. Cool.
2. Stir in lemon juice and strawberries. Pour into an ice-cream container. Freeze in an ice-cream maker according to manufacturer's directions.
3. To serve, make small scoops with a melon baller. Makes 4 servings.

Variation
Substitute any soft fruit or fruit puree for strawberries. As a general guide, use 1 cup unsweetened fruit puree; follow directions above. For an attractive presentation, serve 2 or 3 different flavors. Decorate with a medley of fresh fruit. For example, serve pear, strawberry and raspberry ices with pear slices and 1 or 2 raspberries and strawberries. Or, spoon a little fruit liqueur over top of ices before serving.

Clockwise from top left: Strawberry Ice, Frozen Zabaglione in lemon baskets, Lemon Ice Cream

Praline Ice Cream

Praline:
1/2 cup sugar
3/4 cup unblanched almonds

Custard Base:
1-1/4 cups half and half
1 egg
2 egg yolks
1/2 cup sugar
1-1/4 cups whipping cream

---

1. To make praline, grease a baking sheet. Place sugar and almonds in a saucepan over medium heat until sugar caramelizes. Do not stir. Pour mixture onto greased baking sheet; cool until hard. Grate hard praline with a rotary grater; set aside.
2. In a small saucepan over low heat, bring half and half to a simmer.
3. In a medium, heatproof bowl, beat egg, egg yolks and sugar. Stir in hot half and half; place bowl over a pan of hot water. Cook about 20 minutes or until custard is thick enough to coat back of a spoon, stirring constantly. Cool to room temperature. Refrigerate until cold.
4. In a medium bowl, whip cream until stiff peaks form. Fold into refrigerated custard with 3/4 of praline. Spoon into an ice-cream container. Freeze in an ice-cream maker according to manufacturer's directions.
5. To serve, scoop spoonfuls into a serving dish; sprinkle with remaining praline. Makes 6 servings.

Chestnut Log

8 oz. semisweet chocolate pieces
3/4 cup butter or margarine
2 cups chestnut puree (about 16 oz.)
2 eggs
1 cup sugar
2 tablespoons brandy

To decorate:
Semisweet chocolate, melted
Marrons glacés, if desired

---

1. In a heatproof bowl over hot water, melt 1/2 of chocolate pieces and butter or margarine. Remove from heat; beat in chestnut puree.
2. In a medium bowl, beat eggs and sugar until thick and pale. Beat into chocolate mixture. Stir in brandy and remaining chocolate pieces.
3. Line a 9" x 5" loaf pan with foil or plastic wrap. Spoon chocolate mixture into lined pan. Freeze until almost firm. Remove from pan. Place frozen mixture on a large piece of foil; roll into a log shape. Return to freezer until firm.
4. To serve, place chocolate log on a serving plate. Decorate with melted chocolate and marrons glacés, if desired. Soften at room temperature 15 to 30 minutes before serving. Makes 10 to 12 servings.

Chocolate-Rum Cake

1/2 cup butter or margarine, room temperature
8 oz. semisweet chocolate
1/2 cup sugar
3 eggs
2/3 cup maraschino cherries
1 cup coarsely chopped pecans, almonds or walnuts
2 tablespoons dark rum
1/2 (11-oz.) pkg. tea cookies, broken into pieces

---

1. Grease a 9" x 5" loaf pan. Line pan with waxed paper; grease paper.
2. In a small saucepan over low heat, melt butter or margarine and chocolate until smooth, stirring constantly. Cool.
3. In a medium bowl, beat sugar and eggs until thick and lemon-colored. Gradually stir in cooled chocolate mixture. Stir in cherries, nuts, rum and cookies. Spoon mixture into prepared pan; cover with waxed paper. Freeze several hours or until firm.
4. To serve, invert on a serving plate; remove pan and paper. Place in refrigerator 30 minutes to soften. Makes 12 to 14 servings.

Mississippi Mud Pie

Crumb Crust:
1-1/2 cups chocolate wafer crumbs
1/4 cup butter or margarine, melted

Filling:
1 qt. mocha or coffee ice cream (4 cups)
1 pint double-chocolate ice cream (2 cups)
3 tablespoons coffee-flavored liqueur

Chocolate Sauce:
4 oz. unsweetened chocolate, broken into pieces
1 cup milk or half and half
1/2 cup sugar
1/3 cup light corn syrup
3 tablespoons butter or margarine
1 teaspoon vanilla extract

To decorate:
Sweetened whipped cream
Grated chocolate

This is a simple ice-cream pie served with a warm chocolate sauce.

1. To make crust, in a medium bowl, combine crumbs and butter or margarine until blended. Press crumbs on bottom and up side of a 9-inch pie pan. Freeze until firm.
2. To make filling, in a large bowl, combine mocha ice cream and chocolate ice cream; let stand at room temperature about 15 minutes to soften. Stir in coffee-flavored liqueur until blended. Spoon ice-cream mixture into frozen crust; smooth top. Place in freezer until ice cream is firm.
3. To make sauce, in a medium saucepan over low heat, combine chocolate, milk or half and half, sugar and corn syrup. Cook until chocolate is melted, stirring constantly. Remove from heat; stir in butter or margarine and vanilla. Pour warm sauce into a serving pitcher.
4. Decorate frozen pie with sweetened whipped cream and grated chocolate. Serve with warm Chocolate Sauce. Makes 8 to 10 servings.

Clockwise from top left: Chestnut Log, Praline Ice Cream, Chocolate-Rum Cake

Coffee-Ice-Cream Bombe

1 qt. coffee ice cream (4 cups)
1 pint French-vanilla ice cream (2 cups)
1/2 cup toasted hazelnuts or almonds, finely chopped

To decorate:
1/2 pint whipping cream (1 cup)
Chocolate coffee-bean candies or toasted nuts

1. Place a 1-1/4- or 1-1/2-quart bombe mold or metal bowl in freezer overnight.
2. Reserve 1 cup coffee ice cream for top of mold. Soften remaining coffee ice cream, if necessary.
3. With back of a large spoon, spread coffee ice cream evenly around side and bottom of chilled mold or bowl. Return mold or bowl and remaining ice cream to freezer until firm.
4. In a medium bowl, soften vanilla ice cream; stir in nuts. Pack vanilla-ice-cream mixture in center of coffee-ice-cream-lined mold or bowl, leaving a 1-inch space at top. Freeze again until solid.
5. Soften reserved coffee ice cream; use to fill mold to top. Cover with an oiled circle of waxed paper and a lid. Freeze until firm.
6. To decorate, whip cream until stiff peaks form. Spoon whipped cream into a pastry bag fitted with an open star tip. Refrigerate pastry bag while unmolding bombe.
7. To serve, invert bombe on a serving plate. Wet a dish towel with hot water; wring dry. Wrap towel around mold a few seconds. Carefully remove mold.
8. Decorate bombe with whipped cream. Pipe whipped cream into 2 rows of shell designs across bombe, intersecting rows at top. Pipe stars around base of bombe; pipe a large star where rows of shells meet. Arrange coffee-bean candies or toasted nuts along whipped-cream shells.
9. Serve immediately. Makes 6 to 8 servings.

Coffee-Ice-Cream Bombe

Frozen Lemon Pie

Crust:
3 cups graham-cracker crumbs
1/2 cup butter or margarine, melted

Filling:
8 eggs, separated
Grated peel of 3 lemons
1 cup lemon juice
1 (14-oz. can) sweetened condensed milk
1/2 cup sugar

To decorate:
Whipped cream
Finely shredded lemon peel

---

1. To make crust, in a medium bowl, combine graham-cracker crumbs and butter or margarine. Line bottoms and sides of 2 (9-inch) pie pans with crumb mixture. Refrigerate until firm.
2. To make filling, in a large bowl, beat egg yolks until pale. Stir in lemon peel, lemon juice and condensed milk.
3. In a large bowl, beat egg whites until soft peaks form; gradually beat in sugar. Beat until stiff and glossy. Fold beaten egg-white mixture into lemon mixture. Divide filling between chilled crusts.
4. Freeze until firm. When frozen, wrap pies tightly with plastic wrap and then foil; label. Freeze up to 1 month.
5. Decorate top with small dollops of whipped cream and lemon peel. Makes 2 (9-inch) pies.

Chocolate & Orange Cups

4 oz. semisweet chocolate, melted
1/2 cup whipping cream
2 tablespoons orange-flavored yogurt
2 tablespoons orange-juice concentrate, thawed

To decorate:
Candied orange-peel strips

---

1. Working 1 at a time, pour a little melted chocolate into 6 foil baking cups. Carefully brush a thin layer of chocolate up sides of cups.
2. Refrigerate until firm; then repeat step 1 using remaining chocolate. Refrigerate until firm again. Carefully peel away foil cups. Place chocolate cups on a baking sheet; freeze.
3. To make filling, in a medium bowl, whip cream until stiff peaks form. Fold in yogurt and orange-juice concentrate. Spoon into frozen chocolate cups; swirl tops.
4. Decorate each cup with candied orange-peel strips. Freeze until served. Makes 6 servings.

 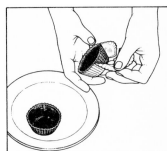

1/Carefully brush chocolate up side of cup.

2/When firm, carefully peel away foil cup.

Chocolate & Orange Cups

Snappy Ginger Sundaes

Snappy Ginger Sundaes

Ginger Horns:
1/4 cup butter or margarine
1/4 cup superfine sugar
2 tablespoons light corn syrup
1/2 cup sifted all-purpose flour
1/2 teaspoon ground ginger
1 tablespoon ginger-flavored brandy or
** syrup from preserved ginger**

Filling:
3/4 cup whipping cream
1 tablespoon powdered sugar
1 qt. vanilla ice cream, or praline ice cream, page 72
Stem ginger preserved in syrup, chopped

1. Preheat oven to 350F (175C). Grease 2 baking sheets.
2. To make Ginger Horns, in a small saucepan, combine butter or margarine, superfine sugar and corn syrup. Stir over low heat until butter or margarine is melted. Remove from heat; stir in flour, ground ginger and brandy or ginger syrup until blended.

3. Using 1 level teaspoon of batter for each cookie, form 3 cookies 3 inches apart on each greased baking sheet. Do not put more than 3 cookies on 1 baking sheet.
4. Place 1 baking sheet at a time in oven; bake 5 to 6 minutes or until cookies are golden brown. Cool on baking sheet 10 seconds. Remove cookies carefully with a wide flat spatula; roll each cookie around a metal pastry horn. Cool completely on a wire rack. When cool, remove metal horn. Repeat to make about 18 cookies.
5. To make filling, in a medium bowl, beat cream until soft peaks form. Beat in powdered sugar; beat until stiff peaks form. Spoon whipped-cream mixture into a pastry bag fitted with an open star tip. Pipe whipped cream into Ginger Horns.
6. Spoon ice cream into 6 tall glasses. Add 2 or 3 filled Ginger Horns; decorate with preserved ginger. Serve immediately. Makes 6 servings.

Mocha-Marshmallow Bombe

1/3 cup dark raisins
1/4 cup golden raisins
1/4 cup currants
1/3 cup pitted, dark sweet cherries, cut into quarters
1/3 cup chopped toasted blanched almonds
3 tablespoons sweet sherry
22 large marshmallows (2-3/4 cups)
2/3 cup milk
1 tablespoon instant coffee powder
1 tablespoon unsweetened cocoa powder
1/2 pint whipping cream (1 cup)
2 tablespoons powdered sugar

---

1. In a medium bowl, combine raisins, currants, cherries and almonds. Stir in sherry. Let stand at room temperature 1 hour.
2. In a medium saucepan, combine marshmallows, milk, coffee powder and cocoa powder. Cook over low heat until marshmallows are melted, stirring constantly. Set aside to cool.
3. In a medium bowl, whip cream until soft peaks form. Beat in powdered sugar; beat until stiff peaks form. Fold in cooled marshmallow mixture. Fold in fruit mixture. Pour into a 6-cup mold; smooth top. Freeze until firm.
4. To serve, invert on a serving plate. Wet a dish towel with hot water; wring dry. Place hot towel around mold a few seconds. Remove mold. Place in refrigerator 20 to 30 minutes to soften before serving. Makes 6 to 8 servings.

Variation
Soften 1 quart of good-quality mocha or coffee ice cream. Stir sherried fruit mixture from step 1 into ice cream. Pack into a 1-quart mold. Freeze until firm.

Nut Tortoni

2 egg whites
1/4 cup sugar
1-1/4 cups whipping cream
1/4 cup amaretto liqueur
1-1/2 cups toasted blanched almonds, coarsely chopped

---

1. In a medium bowl, beat egg whites until soft peaks form. Gradually beat in sugar, 1 tablespoon at a time, until mixture is stiff and glossy.
2. In a medium bowl, whip cream until stiff peaks form. Fold whipped cream into egg-white mixture. Fold in amaretto liqueur and 1/2 of almonds.
3. Spoon mixture into a 9" x 5" loaf pan. Cover and freeze.
4. Invert on a serving plate. Wet a dish towel with hot water; wring dry. Wrap hot towel around pan a few seconds. Remove pan. Press remaining almonds over loaf until completely covered. Freeze again until served. Makes 6 to 8 servings.

Lemon Loaf

1 cup butter or margarine, room temperature
2 cups powdered sugar
Grated peel and juice of 2 large lemons
2 eggs, separated
2/3 cup whipping cream
2 tablespoons Marsala or medium sherry
1 (1-lb.) pound-cake loaf, cut into 3/8-inch slices

To decorate:
Whipped cream
Grated lemon peel

---

1. In a medium bowl, cream butter or margarine, 1-3/4 cups powdered sugar and lemon peel until light and fluffy. Beat in egg yolks, 1 at a time. Beat in 1/2 of lemon juice.
2. In a medium bowl, whip cream until soft peaks form. Fold whipped cream into lemon butter. In a medium bowl, beat egg whites until stiff peaks form. Fold beaten egg whites into lemon mixture.
3. In a small bowl, combine remaining lemon juice and Marsala or sherry. Cover bottom of a 9" x 5" loaf pan with cake slices; sprinkle with a little of Marsala or sherry mixture. Spoon in 1/3 of lemon mixture. Repeat layers ending with cake. There should be 3 layers of lemon mixture and 4 layers of cake. Freeze until served.
4. To serve, invert on a serving plate; remove pan. Decorate with whipped-cream rosettes and grated lemon peel. Allow to soften in refrigerator 30 minutes before serving. Makes 8 servings.

Top to bottom: Mocha-Marshmallow Bombe, Nut Tortoni

Index